ELLERY LITTLETON

RIVERWALK

A POEM A DAY FOR A YEAR

TRAFFORD PUBLISHING, CANADA

Order this book online at www.trafford.com
or email orders@trafford.com

Most Trafford titles are also available at major online book retailers.

Note for Librarians: A cataloguing record for this book is available from Library
and Archives Canada at www.collectionscanada.ca/amicus/index-e.html

Printed in Victoria, BC, Canada.

ISBN: 978-1-4251-8964-8

*Our mission is to efficiently provide the world's finest, most comprehensive book publishing
service, enabling every author to experience success. To find out how to publish your
book, your way, and have it available worldwide, visit us online at www.trafford.com*

Trafford rev. 10/29/2009

 www.trafford.com

North America & international
toll-free: 1 888 232 4444 (USA & Canada)
phone: 250 383 6864 ♦ fax: 812 355 4082

To Mom, Dad & Auntie Dinah

Foreword

On my 65th birthday, I decided to write a poem
a day for a year – a journal in poetry. I needed
a project, and poetry being my favourite form
of writing, it felt like a natural choice. As well,
I wanted the discipline and commitment such a
project requires.

So, on May 3/07, I wrote the first poem; on May
2/08, I wrote the last (366 in all, 2008 being a
leap year). The year passed quickly, and I did, in
fact manage to write a poem for every single day,
although there were times when I felt I couldn't
possibly keep it up. It wasn't until I had written
over half the poems that I began to feel confident
I might actually finish the project.

"I have never started a poem yet whose end I
knew," wrote Robert Frost. "Writing a poem
is discovery." Frost's comment applies to each
poem I wrote. I never really knew where the
writing was leading me, or what to expect.
I had to keep telling myself, "The journey is the
thing; understanding will come later."

Poems are elusive; I seldom had one in mind
when I sat down to write. The best strategy for
me, I discovered, was to simply wait as patiently
as possible for an idea or a feeling to arise. I was
surprised at how well this approach worked.
I would also read other poets, usually Japanese,

looking for inspiration, and allowed myself to write short poems from time to time, with the traditional Japanese haiku as the model. So much can be said in a short poem; three or four lines can effectively capture the mood of a day or the essence of an experience.

On occasion, I would wander far afield, taking mental snapshots, looking for the memorable moment which could be transformed into a poem. I would take my camera along on these journeys - particularly to the rivers, ocean and lakes - and some of the photographs gathered along the way are incorporated throughout the book.

At other times, something would trigger a memory, and I would reach far back into my life to find a poem waiting to be transcribed in present time. As well as being a journal, this book is also something of an autobiography; the past is very present throughout. Hence the dedication to my parents, and my aunt, the family matriarch.

Through the year, I came to see that just below the level of daily awareness the magic realism of poetry flows along like a stream. I found that I could access it by consciously slowing down, breathing, paying attention, opening to myself – meditating, in essence. And I learned in a new way what the abiding concerns and themes of my life are, the elements of my "personal myth" (as Jung called it).

"The interaction with a particular poem becomes a rite of passage from one stage of awareness of self to another, with the poem as the facilitator or guide during the process," writes the novelist Janet Rice. I found this observation to be true for me. The poems led the way; I followed along and did my best to write them down.

"Riverwalk" – the title of the book – is taken from the poem I wrote for June 25/07, after a walk along the Cowichan River, on Vancouver Island.

Ellery Littleton
July, 2008
Victoria, BC

May 3

Sometime after I was born,
early in the morning of May 3,
a nurse brought my mother a cup of tea.
"Best cup of tea I ever had!"
she has said many times over the years,
smiling and shaking her head.
Then she would go on to say
"There was a warm wind blowing,
and I could see the most beautiful
maple tree right outside my window."
This is one of her many stories,
the old familiar songs we all know
by heart that we don't want sung
over and over again.

This morning, however, at breakfast
with my mother, at the beginning of the day
of my birth, it seemed necessary to ask her
to sing the old song once again,
me at sixty-five, her at ninety-one.
The waitress brought tea, and it was weak.
"Not as good as the cup of tea the nurse
brought you after I was born, eh mom," I said.
"Best cup of tea I ever had," she responded
immediately, raising her head, looking out
the window, glancing at me, eyes shining.
"And there was a warm wind blowing,
much warmer than today."
"And the maple tree?" I asked.
"Oh yes," she smiled, far away

for a moment when she was young
and hopeful and twenty-six years old.
"I could see the most beautiful maple tree
right outside my window."

May 4

I am afraid I will always
be afraid.
I love my back yard
and garden.
I am afraid I will never shake
the blues.
I love this luscious bursting
spring afternoon.
I am afraid I will lose
my edge, my will, my memory,
my wallet, my driver's licence,
my goddamn social insurance
number, my marbles!

I can still remember ...
the phone number we had at home
over fifty years ago: 1080-X
(pronounced "one-oh-eight-oh-ex").
in the little house on Beaver Creek Road.
I remember the exact sound
of my new basketball ringing
as it hit the hard-packed earth
out beside the old garage
where I had my hoop.

I am afraid the first thing
I will always say when I get up
in the morning will be "ah shit."
I'm afraid I won't have
fun any more.

May 5

My friend called from France today
to wish me a happy birthday,
a couple of days late, as usual.
I haven't seen him for ten years.
We talked about our lives, like old
friends do: children, work, weather,
the habits of the French, mutual
acquaintances and their misfortunes,
books we had read, our feelings about
aging, because he is a Taurus too.
Two years younger than me, he once
called me his older brother. I have almost
forgotten his infuriating eccentricities.
I hope he has forgotten mine.

May 6

Half asleep in the
hot morning sun
I am jolted awake
by a sudden buzz and

flutter right beside my ear.
Flapping and flailing, heart
pounding, I welcome the first
hummingbird of the year.

May 7

The arc of a day:
slow in the early morning,
faster in the late morning
and early afternoon.
Slow in the late afternoon
and early evening.
Dead slow in the later evening.
Sort of a soft bell curve
of a day.
And along the way on this
bell curve of a day, a passionate
red rhododendron, delicate pink
and white tulips, purple lilac
blossoms, with a scent like
freshly pressed grape juice.
And so much more.

May 8

Both faces of Chen Mu'an,
the god with two hearts,
appear most frequently
in the art of the ancient

and mysterious dynasty
of the Han.

Cast in bronze,
carved in wood,
sculpted in stone,
rustic and rough
to the north,
cultured and smooth
to the south,
with one bare foot
in the river
and one bare foot
on the sand
he stands between
the two worlds.

Offerings for Mu'an
must be carried
in both hands.
For his left side,
rope and roots,
brown rice and stones,
pepper and ginger,
ginseng and garlic,
black mountain tea
and poppy seeds.
For his right side,
mother of pearl,
polished sandalwood,
Tibetan incense,
bamboo wind chimes,
a green jade cup

of cold water
from the temple well,
and white bone marble
of the moon.

Chen Mu'an speaks
to the ancestors
of light and dark,
of life after death,
of reincarnation and rebirth.

When the influences of Chen
are in harmony in a man
he will live – not like a god –
but like a pilgrim
on the shining path
to Heaven.

For Bill Yeomans (1918-2006)

May 9

I read the obituaries these years.
Sometimes I see an old familiar
face in a faded photograph
appearing for a day or two,
then gone, as they used to say,
to a better place.

Family and friends.
Many have made the final move
out and away in recent years,
abandoned houses in declining
neighborhoods; once there was life
now there are memories.

And yet, as I sit
on my back yard bench
the sun is warm on my
writing arm and birds are
competing with shrill music,
but music nevertheless.
Light and shadow falls across
the lawn, and the bamboo
whispers as my wife moves
through the garden,
pouring water, pulling weeds.

May 10

A beautiful spring evening.
Again, the animated chatter
of birds on all sides. And again,
the subject of obituaries comes up.
Wholly unexpected, a request
from my friend's wife,
asking me to write his.
"It was in his will," she said.
"He wanted you to do it."

So many gaps in the jigsaw
of a long and diverse life.
I only have a few pieces;
the rest is a series of ragged
blank spaces, with the tablecloth
showing through underneath.
From the oft-shuffled pack
of pictures from the past
I draw one card. I am travelling
to Hornby Island, circa 1982,
to visit Bill in his zen temple
cabin high on the hill, deep
in the forest. It is early autumn,
warm and dry. There is a heap
of freshly bucked firewood
by the back porch. Bill offers me
his long-handled axe and asks me
to split some wood, please,
before dinner, and stack it
over there, beneath the stairs.

He has his shirt off, belt cinched
tight. He is tanned and fit,
with long ropes of muscle,
and hands as big as catcher's mitts.
He smells of garlic and sweat
and tobacco. He lights his pipe
and stands in the shade, smoking
reflectively, watching me work,
nodding with approval.
One of the reasons he likes me,
I know, is because I am willing
to work for my dinner.

May 11

Stories about friends who have died
are always stories about ourselves.
I noticed this today at the memorial
for Bill. Those who spoke told
their own stories, intertwined
with their memories of Bill.
But their own stories came first,
about how he affected their lives:
"I first met Bill …"
and out it would come,
about the friend, the companion,
the mentor, the father figure,
the rascal, the trickster,
the warrior, the clown.
That's what a death will do for you.
It allows you to step forward

and tell one of your own stories,
a story you might otherwise
keep to yourself, a story
you would tell by candlelight,
seated at your old desk upstairs,
deep in the dead of night.

May 12

My greed has made me
look my age. In the mirror
I see the one eye that droops
a little when I'm tired.

It's all been said,
everybody knows,
it's folk knowledge,
life begins at 60.
You're not getting older,
the best is yet to come,
but the end of the road
could be just around the bend
and we're picking up speed,
so it seems.
I should have booked
my passage in advance
in order to avoid surprises.

I wash my cup.
I dry my hands.
I walk outside

into the cool starlight
of a spring night.
My grown children are asleep
in their own beds, far away,
breathing deep and slow, I know.
The air is sweet with flower scent
drifting from the park.

Somewhere a dog barks,
a door slams, a yellow lamp
spills light like molten butter
through the dark.
Thin white clouds float
across the new moon
and I can feel the slow motion
of the globe rolling round
the hidden midnight sun.

Why do children think
they will live forever?
The most powerful illusion
of all comes with the gift of life.

May is the month
of shooting stars this year ...
three seconds of silver fire
and they're dead.
I burn more slowly
than the stones that fall
from space. I love the light
my moving life creates.

May 13

Finally, I give myself the gift
of a few minutes outside on this
warm and fragrant afternoon
in the oasis of the back yard
to sit under the oak on my
favourite bench and write
myself a poem.

I see more green and blue
than I can comprehend.
I hear distant drums:
marching bands practicing
for the parade; a train
whistle in the distance,
calling to me of childhood.
I smell sweet azaleas
and my neighbor's dinner
on the barbecue.
I feel the cool fresh wind
from the west, from the sea,
the oracle of rain rushing
through the trees.
I can almost taste
the red Chilean wine
I am saving for tonight.

Damn! There goes my neighbor
mowing his lawn. The harsh
song of the season roaring
not fifty feet away. I can't

write a poem under these
circumstances. That's it
for today. Pisses me off.

May 14

(To my father, on his birthday)

Somewhere on this river
half-way between the lake
and the sea, his spirit suddenly
appeared, hovering like a dragonfly
on a soft spring breeze.

"Here it is!" I shouted silently,
I know how you loved
the late afternoon light,
the rippling, chattering musk
and mud-scented river
flowing west to the sea,
the sense of forever
in the optimistic clouds,
buoyant in the eggshell sky,
the lush and dusky evergreen
carpet of old growth rolling
across the ridge and all the
incredible way up the valley
to the smoke and snow
of Forbidden Plateau.

Alas, these visions of perfection
and moments of boundless
expectation never last for long.
Did you find that? I know you did.
Because I remember you before
and after your surrender.

Well, I'm still here
and I felt you here too
living through me today,
immersed for a moment
in my sweet deep childhood
dream of the green and golden
grove, the slanting sun, warm
sand by the edge of the stream,
mottled rocks beneath the water
like so many ancient eggs.
Somewhere downstream
the dinner bell rings,
and we run happily
hungrily home.

May 15

It's raining today,
heavy, persistent and gray.
Oh hell … might as well
clean the house, turn inward,
away from the sullen afternoon.

I vacuum the carpets in the hall,
sweep the kitchen and wash the floor,
give the bathroom a thorough reaming,
including the toilet, tub and sink,
kowtowing before the porcelain god.
Humble chores indeed, another version
of the old zen thing about washing
my bowl, drawing water, hewing wood,
being the royal road to awareness.
I don't know about that,
but I do know it has to be done.
Cleaning the toilet, I mean.

May 16

From the dentist's chair
I can see for miles.
Trees just across the road
bending in the wind.
Headlights flashing on the
highway, blue mountains
half-hidden in the distance.
A seagull soaring

past the window.
I close my eyes.
I am in another place
far away.

May 17

My green friend is pale,
sickly-hued, and jealous,
yes.

Unripe, young and tender,
not dried, seasoned or tanned,
true.

Immature? Yes.
Also undeveloped,
inexperienced and gullible,
fresh and not healed.
Loves unripe cheeses,
turtle fat (esteemed by epicures),
the plums of Sir William Gage,
the apples of Granny Smith,
the woodlands in the summer
and the outlaw life.

Builds little glass houses
for his garden of moss,
peas and shamrocks.
Collects feldspar,
hornblende and jade.

Takes tea
at the gaming table,
plays billiards and croquet,
bowls, putts and punts
on the grassy public plain.
Wears an emerald in his navel
and a glove on the thumb
of his green right hand.
My green friend ...
how he grows on me!

May 18

My daughter flew to Hawaii today.
My son flies to California tomorrow.
They are 33 and 35 years old
respectively, with a total
of 68 years of life
between them altogether.
You would think that by now
I would have stopped
worrying about them.
And I have, sort of.
But old habits die hard,
to coin a phrase.
And although I too
may die hard,
it damn well better be
before my children.

May 19

The long drive from Victoria to
Tofino, so familiar, yet always fresh.
The landscape changing through the year
from green to yellow to brown to gray
and back to green again. Long after
I am gone the landscape will still be
changing, year after year, season after
season. I can't even imagine how
it will look a hundred years from now.
A hundred years ago there was no road
over the mountains and out to the sea.
Back then, there were forests forever
and more fish than you could dream
of catching. All different now.
Forests falling away, fish almost gone,
and tourists come just to watch the waves
in winter while dining in the posh café.

May 20

Sitting at a paint-stained table
in Ken's studio, looking out
through the trees to the beach,
surf thundering, fog gathering
far offshore. Soon Ken will move
back to the city and this old growth
outpost will be closed forever.
The end of another era. Not a
large one, but an era nevertheless.

One by one, they come to a close,
like waves on the beach of eternity,
washing away all that was yesterday.

"You're not looking as limber as
you used to be," Heather says.
And I'm not. Not as limber,
and not as I used to be.

Once again, my list of "shoulds"
comes up as I face into my inevitable
aging and decline. I should eat less,
exercise more, do more yoga, bite back
on my bad habits. Easier said than done.
I know, because I've often said
and seldom done. But maybe I can
grow older with some grace and style,
sense of humour roughly intact.
I guess I'll give it a whirl.
Meanwhile, the mother-of-pearl
early evening light lies like a coat
of fresh lacquer on the shining sand.

May 21

A warm late spring
afternoon, muggy and close.
Gentle breezes stir the trees
in my yard and keep me cool.
Machine noises strafe
the neighborhood:

power saw, lawn mower,
leaf blower, rumbling car,
hip-hop thundering,
driven by a white teenager,
with a nodding bobble-head.

Suddenly there is room
for the softer sounds:
someone sweeping, birds
chattering, children laughing
in the park, the distant tinkling
of the ice cream vendor's van.

I'm not at the peak
of my apex today,
as my father used to say.
My energy is low,
my wits are slow,
my head aches,
my gut is sour
(shouldn't have had that
extra cup of coffee with
breakfast after all).
My ambition is flagging,
my humour is sagging,
I'm dragging myself
through the day.
But would I rather be
anywhere else?
No way.

May 22

I'm keeping my inner poet busier
than he's ever been, asking him to
write poems every week for a year.
He groans when he gets up from
the couch and slouches into the
writing room where his pen and
paper lie passively on the table.
"You can't wait for inspiration,"
Jack London said. "You have to
go after it with a club."

My inner poet is different
than he was in the past. Then,
it was all about creating cleverly
constructed artifacts, jewelry for
discerning customers. The tools
required for this diamond cutter's
approach to poem-making are like
jewels themselves, small, sharp,
strong, shining under the brilliant light
and the magnifying glass. There was
really no need for the cumbersome club
in this array of refined implements,
perfect, in their way, like German-
crafted optical instruments.

But in order to write one poem
a day, my inner poet has gone
down to the basement and out
into the back forty where he has
collected several humble garden
tools to add to his big old sack of

scribbler's tricks: a hoe, a rake,
a shovel, a hammer, an axe.
And yes, a club as well, leaning
against the wall next to the shears,
for the heavy work that needs doing
now and then. Sometimes something
has to be cut off, or simply
beaten into submission.

May 23

In a previous incarnation
I must have worked in a zen
temple, sweeping and raking,
forms of moving meditation.
Leaves fallen from the trees
of autumn, summer grasses,
spring petals, dry winter dirt,
all must be gathered up care-
fully and deposited discreetly
out of sight. The challenge is
to create the illusion that all
is neat, orderly and controlled.
Perfection is not the goal,
however. There must be a
flaw in the arrangement to
make the feng shui interesting.
Two leaves on the sand,
red and gold; three strands
of yellow grass across the path;
four pink petals and five white,
just right under the cherry tree.

May 24

Pink and blue and white,
red and green and striped,
sheets and pillow cases,
shirts and sweaters,
pyjamas and peddle-pushers,
socks and underwear,
they're all there, humble
flags gently flapping on my
new neighbour's clothesline.
I heard it before I saw it.
An old familiar scraping,
a nagging, throat-clearing,
cranky, irritating sort of sound,
squealing for lubrication,
a small sound from the past,
before all my aunts and uncles died,
when you got to see and hear
your neighbours in their back yards
every day, women on their toes,
stretching to put the clothes pegs on,
white legs poking out from
under flowered house dresses,
rushing to subdue the flailing
long johns, dancing with St. Vitus
in a sudden breeze.
From my kitchen window
I watched my new neighbour
gathering in her freshly-dried
laundry this afternoon.
She moved deliberately,

with ease and care, within
her own clearly delineated space.
She folded each piece
as though it were precious
and old, smoothing out
the wrinkles before laying it
gently in her basket. We might
be good neighbours, I thought.
We have something in common.

May 25

cautious crows
patient crows
sometimes wait
for hours before
swooping down
to snatch the bread
I have scattered
on the grass.

May 26

After dinner this evening
I am sitting on the bench
in the back yard, notebook
on my lap, holding my pen
in my left hand, waiting
for inspiration.
It feels like it will be
a long wait. Although
the evening is beautiful
(perhaps a little cool)
with the surround sound
of a thousand birds singing
in a sweet, ragged choir,
the lawn smooth and elegant
calling for croquet, the garden
bursting with flowers,
the potato patch rising
like a miniature rain forest
(I can almost hear the spuds
rustling underground,
clamouring to be mashed
boiled or baked).

I am not sure I have a poem
in mind. Suddenly, my wife
emerges from the house for her
evening garden tour, pausing
to toss some limp greens into
the compost and pick a few
leaves from the catnip plant

to give to our two old felines
who have followed her
on her rounds in hopes of
receiving just such a treat.

Still no poem.
I'm tired tonight.
I don't know why.
I guess I'll go back inside
and have another cup of tea.
Oh, I hear the phone ringing.
I wonder if it's for me?

May 27

To be alive is to be dirty.
On what should be
another perfect spring day,
I am preoccupied
with this elemental truth.

There are nests of
tiny green worms
suspended in our apple tree.
Voracious little buggers,
they turn the leaves brown
and make a mess on
the ground below.
As always, the dust gathers
and must be swept away
from the basement door

and off the front porch,
along with the woodbugs,
spiders and ants, all scuttling
desperately, looking for
another grubby little oasis
in which to set up camp.
The bathroom floor also needs
sweeping; same for the kitchen.
I'll bag up some garbage
as well and dump the compost.
The car must be washed
and the crap taken out
of the trunk. And I should
jump in the shower before
going out, but really I
don't have time.

May 28

(I Ching reading - #42 – Increase)

The judgment:
"increase."
It furthers one to
undertake something.
It furthers one to
cross the great water.

Wind and thunder;
the image of increase.
Thus, the superior man,

sees good and integrates it;
has faults, and rids himself
of them.

Confucius says:
the superior man sets his person
at rest before he moves; composes
his mind before he speaks; makes
his relations firm before he asks
for something. This way, he gains
complete security.

But if a man is brusque
in his movements, others
will not co-operate.
If he is agitated in his words,
they awaken no echoes in others.
If he asks for something without
having first established relations,
it will not be given to him.
If no one is with him, those who
would harm him draw near.

May 29

wild wind!
wind chimes crashing

wind subsides ...
wind chimes silent

wild wind!

May 30

the neighbour's cat
sneaks through my garden
and jumps over the fence
before I can nail him
with this lump of dirt
I have been saving.

May 31

beautiful May
luscious May
hard to let her go ...
if I could persuade her
to stay forever
I would too
I know.

June 1

the neighbour's dog
poops on my lawn . . .
later I scoop it up
and throw it back
where it belongs.

June 2

"You're so serious," she says.
"You should lighten up."
"I've heard that before . . .
too many times and I've
said it to myself over and
over again, like verbal prayer
beads, a mantra of sorts, to help
deflect the power of negative thinking.
Anyway, how can I not be so serious?
It's the way I am; it's the way things are,
all that bullshit coming down.

June 3

It was unusually wet
this spring, I am told.
I don't know. I guess
I missed it. But now that

I pay attention, I can almost
hear the grass rustling as it
grows, like a layer of plankton
in the nutrient ocean,
writhing in slow motion.

June 4

Looking outside at nothing,
not so much lost in thought
as simply sitting, still and silent.
Suddenly, a bird shoots past
the window, just a blur, a streak,
a line on the retina dashed off
with the finest of brushes.
Now I am standing, thinking
out loud, making a cup of tea.
What a difference a bird makes.

June 5

Tuesday's wind
tears in from the west,
cold, uncaring and selfish.
Just wants to mess things up,
bust a few branches and
make people miserable,
make 'em gripe about
the goddamn weather and
how late spring was this year.

Get used to it people!
Spring never was the same,
and never will be again.

June 6

morning sneeze
freaks the
neighbor's cat.

June 7

Sluggish morning ...
I feel stiff, fat & old.
Sounds like partners
in a law firm.
Which one would you hire?

June 8

This friggin' lawnmower
weighs a ton, and I'm sweatin'
like a pig in the mornin' sun.
I got the late overweight
middle-age honkie blues.

June 9

Like warm, plump children
cradled gently in my arms,
two loaves of fresh bread
from the Italian bakery,
whole wheat and sourdough.

June 10

A very long lost distant cousin
comes to town and calls me.
We met only once, fifty years ago,
and even now I can see her
standing tall in my aunt's
fragrant kitchen, long black hair
falling down her back, blue eyes
shining. I was smitten ...
my American cousin,
so beautiful and cool.

June 11

I've had quite a run of dreamtime
blockbusters lately, including a few
appearances by my dark-eyed
Shadow Guy, who has been eschewing
his familiar Iago routine. Last night,
for instance, he took the romantic lead,
handsome and young, seductive in an Italian

sort of way, acting like Animus in love,
needing a shave and a haircut, and
probably a bath. I introduced him
to my Anima; they're about the same
age and look fabulous together.

June 12

Like giant noisy killer bees,
weed–whackers buzz-bomb
the neighbourhood.

June 13

My neighbour
is a mowing fool.
Whatever it is,
he's taking it out
on the grass.

June 14

Today, an extraordinary
ordinary day.
Sleeping in a little.
A light breakfast
and one cup of tea.
Some notes in

my poetry journal.
Some gifts unwrapped
at the kitchen table.
Some work in the garden.
A drive to the bank
and the grocery store.

A longer drive in the country,
stopping for a scrumptious
lunch in a chardonnay yellow
restaurant on the way to buy
two overflowing hanging plants
for the back yard.

Then home again, home again,
not jiggedy-jig, exactly,
but in a leisurely fashion,
sleepy from the wine and food
and the ritual sniffing of roses.
A quick nap, a quick shower,
then coffee and carrot cake
with mother, sister, brother-
in-law, son, friend, and wife,
whose birthday it is today.

This woman of sixty,
born in forty-seven,
married for thirty-eight,
still looks like the sweet
child of six in the photo
on our bedroom table.

June 15 (dream poem)

Carrying my bags, with one eye
on the clock, I am walking through
an airport or a ferry terminal,
one of those eternal corridors,
the archetypal journey between
here and there, now and then.
In the river of people flowing
both ways, I gently collide with
a young woman heading down-
stream, and as we apologize
to each other, I notice with a start
that she is carrying my notebook,
my precious poetry journal.
She says she found it and is happy
to return it to me. I look closely at
her face which is strong and clear,
without makeup.
"You're First Nations, aren't you,"
I say. She nods, looking directly
at me in a not unfriendly way.
"I'm going home," she replies,
"to Haida Gwai."
Visions of totem poles in
the rainforest, cloud-shrouded
mountains descending to the sea,
long black canoes gliding down
the coastline; the distant sound
of drums in the longhouse,
the wild chant of the women
soaring into the night sky with
the smoke from the cooking fire.

Suddenly she is gone, swept
away in the current of the crowd.
And I continue on upstream,
cradling my book of poems
(which I did not know I had lost)
next to my heart.

June 16

Every day now
I am on the alert
for the elusive poem.
Will it be the hour
in the bookstore,
where I could have spent
a thousand dollars easily?
It might be the disagreeable
telephone conversation I had
with the magazine editor.
It could easily be the agreeable
hour I spent with a friend
over coffee at a sidewalk café.
It will probably be about
watering the garden.
Hose in hand, I wandered,
feeling like a passing shower,
a giant looming over the rainforest.
Thoughts came and went
and I let them go, flotsam
on the stream of consciousness.
I felt, heard and smelled

the world around me:
hot sun, lawnmowers,
sirens in the distance,
the scent of wild roses.
The poems are out there,
I know. Like butterflies
they must be captured gently
in the cupped hands
of my imagination.

June 17

Garage band practicing
in the decrepit house
across the street.
Or is that the demolition
crew? Hard to tell.

June 18 (dream poem)

"Ellery McGee – is that really your name?"
The fat detective giggled at me.
I could smell cigarette smoke
coming off him like poison gas.

"Yes it is," I said. "And is your name
really Lard Ass?"

His ugly mug collapsed from a smirk
into a sullen scowl. "Better watch yourself
asshole," he grunted, "cause we'll be watching
you."

Sounds like vintage Mickey Spillane,
I thought. I'll bet he's used it a thousand
times before. I slammed the door as he
lumbered down the stairs, then sat and
lowered my head into my hands,
holding it in place.

June 19 (dream poem)

Looking back now, I wonder
how I could have been so stupid.
Sucker punched by love,
I believed everything she told me
and fell happily into the tantric
trance, mouth wide open.
She could spot a sugar junkie
a mile away, and slipped me

some of the straight stuff
as soon as she got close enough
to see who I really was.

I am looking back now;
we are at her villa in Mexico,
high on the hill above the sea.
She leaves early in the morning
while I am still asleep.
Just packs up and breezes out
without waking me, which is
amazing, seeing as how I could be
the world's lightest sleeper.
When I come to, she is gone.
Not a note, not a clue, just a hint
of her exotic perfume clinging
to my skin like essential oil ...
looking back now ... it is almost
tropical ... almost sensual ...
... almost blue.

June 20

Sister solstice arrived today
without a fanfare or a fuss,
a passenger on the mid-day
bus from Gemini to Cancer.
A tourist from the south
in a Polynesian skirt,
she sauntered off toward
the bay, and on the way
she kissed me on the mouth.

June 21

Why is it whenever I sit
down to write a poem I think
I have to be profound?

Why not write about simple
things in simple ways?
Like the reflection
of the Japanese maple
in our little back yard pool.

But then, it's alright to write
about profound things too,
like the reflection
of the Japanese maple
in our little back yard pool.

June 22

Carelessly raking
I knock a blossom
from our little apple tree.
With death occurring
on all levels, at all times,
everywhere, why should
this bother me?
Just a simple blossom
bursting with life on the
lush green grass of summer.

June 23

I dream of the lake, the cooling
womb of summer, when it's hot
like this, and the ultimate high
season pleasure — falling off the dock
through space for one brief moment
of exquisite and terrifying anticipation
before the all-consuming plunge into
the cold water, which soon becomes
cool water, thank God, cool enough
to take the edge off the blistering heat
and save my feet from the burning boards.
At times like this, you can tell me to go
soak my head, baby, and I will.

I have a favourite photo of myself
taken at the lake by my wife a couple
of years ago. I did not know she had
caught me as I lay clinging to the ladder,
the back of my head in the water, eyes
closed, a typical space for me, half in
the light, conscious of my surroundings,
half submerged in the darkness, almost
black in the photo, my head reflected
in undulating waves, unconscious
like the lake itself.

Photo by Mary Helen Littleton

June 24

My son flew off
to California today.
I felt a little like
I used to feel when
he went to the hospital
or the high school
or the summer camp.
So much brutality
in various forms,
from the infinitely
sharp and subtle to
the football-in-the-face
version of adolescent
cruelty. He needed a
little more protection,
I used to feel. Anyway,
I had no choice; I had to
step forward; love and fear
required it. Maybe I
over-protected him.
Maybe not.
But as he disappeared into
the terminal this morning,
a big guy, carrying his bags
with ease, his buddy by his
side, I felt so much love
for him, with a bitter dash
of the old sorrow, that I sat
behind the wheel of my car
and wept before heading for
the highway home again

June 25

Driving south
through the lights
over the bridge
my tired eyes
catch sight of river
down and to the right.

Just a glimpse
a reflection
gliding on glass
a slippery green glitter
beneath the canopy
of summer trees
is all I need.
River reaches up to me
dashes water in my face
and washes down my frown.

Over the bridge
along the dirt road
out of the car
into the light …
the air is wet with scent.

The highway calls
like distant surf
but here birds chatter
dappled sunlight dazzles
through the leaves
and I smell river.

Musk and mud
rotting leaves
sweet skunk cabbage
and just a touch of trout
drying on the sand.

I remember this smell
when rivers were creeks
and I hung from branches
over swimming holes.
Some things grow so well
in fields beside rivers ...
wild strawberries
long grass, maple trees
and the sons of
small town folk.

Through the branches
I see it now
spider webs shine
with morning dew
my running shoes
are soaked and
river is mine.
Wide and shallow
seamless and swift
liquid jade
shooting blues
molten watercolours
flowing by.
My eyes jump
like skipping stones
across the surface

to the other side.
What are these tears?
My heart is pounding.
I am grateful and
say my thank you's
to the green god of rivers.

An invisible deity
he moves on breezes
that sweep upstream
showers where the rapids
boil, sneaks up on me
and with a ripple, takes me
by the memory and soaks
me in sweet mysteries.
I strip off my clothes
and throw myself at river
like a jealous needful lover.
I am white like the rocks
that bite my city feet.
The racing stones
slippery as soap
are no place for a
naked man, dancing
like a fool on ice.

My blood races
my skin shrinks
my bones are exposed.
I will be bleached
by the sun on a gravel
bank, burnt by children

kicked and scattered
like sticks into the gentle
arms of the river god
and swept away forever.

June 26

Don't worry spiders,
woodbugs and crickets,
I wield my summer broom
casually. But earwigs …
so sorry, no place for you.

June 27

The heady scent of roses
all around. The sound
of laughter rising
from nearby tables.

The taste of cold
white wine and
fresh french bread.
Warm sun, dappled shade
beneath the trees,
the light blue sea
stretching away to islands
in the summer haze.
A garden café day
dream lunch with you.

June 28

A day of sensory delights.
A crate of fresh local strawberries,
each one a sunburst of summer
flavour. Wild roses, tiny and pink,
exuding champagne bubbles
of scent fit for a forest sprite.
A view across the bay from
a bench under a spray of yellow
broom. Memories of seasons
long gone down the path to the
beaches of yesterday when the
afternoon sun was a little too hot,
the breeze not quite cool enough,
and everything delicious, including
the girl in the blue bathing suit
which was bluer than her eyes,
bluer even than the sky, bluer
than my adolescent heart.

June 29

Driving north on holiday
into the deep nostalgic flow
of poignant memories,
summer dreams, bittersweet
and salty, reflections of a time
when desire touched everything,
and hearts broken in the dark
were healed in the light.

June 30

Moon, spoon, croon, swoon ...
all those June words echoing
through the trees above the beach,
mantras from the Isle of Circe
just offshore. I wanted everything
they promised when I was seventeen.
I wanted something ...something more ...
something else ... something as luscious
as a ripe peach and tangy as a secret word
laden with intimation. I wanted something
then ... I want it now. What can it be?
A dream ... just a dream of innocence.

July 1

Summer evening,
silent and mild.
I tip-toe across
the dew-soaked lawn
to stand in the light
of the crescent moon.
Tonight, even the stars
are whispering.

July 2

Gleaming in the light
from the kitchen window,
sixteen jars of freshly-made
jam. Raspberry, loganberry,
liquid ruby red, the life blood
of summer for the depths
of winter to spread like
heaven's manna
on dark Italian bread.

July 3

The city is a monster
with concrete tentacles,
alive with metal and too
much of everything.
It's exciting, like a shot
of speed, but no place
for a small town boy like me.
My little old home town, on the
other hand, is still something
of a clearing in the wilderness.
There is one busy corner where
the local traffic jam takes place
twice a day for half an hour,
but a stone's throw from the
mini-mall and you're all
alone on a green river flowing
out of a blue lake past yellow
fields and sun-stained farmhouses
on the way to the long arm
of the sea.

I know who I am in the old home town,
where necks are red and collars blue
and there's not a decent restaurant
to be found. Life is so much simpler
there, at least in terms of getting around.
I started there and I'll probably end up
there, somehow, closer to the ground.

July 4

Before bed I will have
one last walk through
this still soft summer night.

Across the field and up
the hill, black bushes
don't bother me,
I'm invulnerable and free,
singing silently, "I am open
to the night, I am open
to the night."

At the top of the hill,
under the sweeping net
of sky filled with living light,
I hear movie music rising round
the lovers parked and purring.
Sweet and sticky, it clings to me
like a daughter's first perfume.
Anima rising, boyhood dreams
reviving, aegean eyes, the ocean
and the moon.

Down the other side
to the bench above the beach,
I lie in wait for shooting stars.
One! Two! And finally three,
enough for just one summer walk.

July 5

It's not always easy to find
holy ground. But once you're
hidden in the secret grove
of cedars, kneeling before the
flickering fire, you can call upon
the spirits to blow smoke into
the eyes of the everyday world.

July 6

New clothes for summer;
blue shorts and a white shirt.
Oh-oh … too tight!

July 7

A herbal de-tox cleanse.
Oh dear! No more bread
and wine. For a while.

July 8

Looking back thirty-six years,
almost to the day. Early July, 1971.
two ferry trips from Campbell River
to Cortes Island, the most northerly of
that bonsai archipelago along the east
coast of Vancouver Island, far out there
somewhere. We are on our way to a
five-day workshop with Alan Watts at
the Cold Mountain Institute, a "growth center"
(a 60's sort of phrase; a 60's sort of place)
crossed with a new age zen monastery,
on the rim of the Pacific, facing east.
Organic food, rocky beaches, islands
hovering in the strait, mountains
in the distance. Sitting on the deck,
drinking coffee, we watch the sun set over
the largest Japanese garden in the universe.
Watts is a philosophical entertainer
with theatrical flair, wily and wise,
rakish and wild, boozing and smoking
black cheroots, a pirate with a silver earring,
a Shakespearian rapscallion, a Zen Sensualist,
a monk, a shaman, an artist, a poet, a shrink
of sorts, and an aristocratic gentleman
of the old school. I look back with nostalgia
and a yearning for the optimism and sheer
heady possibility of things which coloured
that hopeful, thrilling time.
Watts died two years later, only fifty-eight.
Fell deep asleep, and did not wake up.

Richard Weaver told me. Richard,
the resident guru and human potential
heavyweight at Cold Mountain, a Papa
Hemingway kind of guy, with a brilliant
eye for body language, and an ear
for the bullshit and the truth.

"Alan was bored to death," Richard said.
"He felt he'd seen it all, and had had enough."

July 9

There are two sides to the coin
of feeling alone; heads or tails,
it all depends on the day.
Heads you win.
You enjoy feeling alone.
You take time for your self,
and your self needs
some time with you.
You rake the lawn.
You go for a walk.
You avoid long conversations.
You don't make any plans
for the evening, and spend
an hour or two reading
a good book. You go to bed
early and sleep like a baby,
because you are a baby
in this state of grace, cradled
in the arms of Morpheus.
Tails you lose.
You are lonely.
You have too much
time on your hands,
and it weighs heavy.
You're too tired
to go for a walk.
You want to call somebody,
but you don't know who.
Everybody is busy anyway,
and nobody loves you.

You crash in front of the t.v.
and go to bed late.
You sleep wretchedly;
it's too hot; dark dreams
ebb and flow on the tide
of your unconscious.
That's sort of the way
it goes in this life.

July 10

Another Saturday, a day of doing,
not thinking. Well, not thinking
as much as I might on a Tuesday
or a Thursday, which are days
for reflecting, not doing.
Days have personalities, after all,
and Saturday is a working fool,
A-type and driven, bustling
around, getting things done.
In the morning, I tended the garden,
watering obsessively, wandering
restlessly, looking for things
to clean up: tiny apples fallen
prematurely from the tree,
destined for an early trip
to the compost; dirt, leaves,
dust, bugs, dead flowers,
cobwebs and birdshit,
the detritus of the world
which falls like invisible

dandruff on everything.
And later in the afternoon,
after a brief snooze and
a cup of tea (well, two cups
actually, and a cookie), a trip
to the grocery store, standing
in line cheek-by-jowl with people
who would normally not have
anything to do with me,
all of us being nice Canadians,
polite, patient and bored.
Then a birthday dinner
for my friend, accompanied
by his sparkling red-haired
daughter, a nurse (lucky people
who get Jill on the psychiatric ward).
My wife baked a Somass River salmon,
served with curry ginger sauce, along
with hot potatoes from our garden
and cold Chardonnay. And, of course,
a splendidly obese birthday cake,
positively bursting with delicious calories.
I had two pieces (the second was quite
small, really) and a cup of coffee with
whipping cream. After clearing up
the dishes and watching an hour of
junk t.v., I crept off to bed feeling fat
and happy in that Saturday sort of way.

July 11

Back in the saddle again, on the trail
to the lake. Three days only in a cabin
in the trees, a brief sojourn in the oasis
by the big water. Arriving at noon,
my wife and I, hot from the road
and a little stiff, stand on the deck
listening to the chuckling and sloshing
of the waves, the bumping of boats
and docks, like restless cattle in the barn,
the wind sighing through the trees,
fragments of family business overheard
from nearby houses, outboard motors
buzzing like wasps, next door,
then far away, fading into silence.

Finally, we tug on our bathing suits,
the universal uniforms of summer,
and meander down the path to the dock,
sunscreen, hats and towels in hand,
and offer ourselves to the sunshine,
the wind, the wide open spaces
all around us, above, below, south,
east and west. Only north is held
at bay, behind a range of mountains
and the tilting of the globe.

Back up on the deck, in and out
of our little cabin, there is time
to sit, to read, to play solitaire,
to write journal entries and poems,

trying, with mixed results, to capture
the elusive enchantment of ordinary
days made extraordinary, in part, by
the fact that there won't be many more.

July 12

My first swim in the lake
this year. I lie in the hot sun
until I have to take the plunge.
So cold at first! So cool
in a moment. So perfect
after that. Soon, I'll do it
all over again.

July 13

Neighbors at the lake are noisy.
To be alive is to make noise in these
gas-powered parts, it seems.
Motorboats, water bombers,
chain saws, children screaming,
someone's favorite golden
oldies blaring in the afternoon.
To seek silence and the natural
sounds of wind and water
is deemed a peculiar affectation
in this red neck of the valley,
apparently.

July 14

Mid-summer swaggered in today
with a blast of heat from the barbecue.
How do you like your sunburn?
Rare, medium or well-done?
I do love summer, but too much
of a good thing is not, as
Mae West said, wonderful.
Although ... ask me about this
come November; I may have
a different point of view.

July 15

It's all going on without me
in my yard and garden.
Flowers are blooming and dying,
fading to brown, dust to dust,
then it's deja vu next summer again,
reincarnation in red and blue.
Sitting quietly in my chair
in the afternoon shade, I am aware
of the exquisitely complex layers
of life all around me, radiating
out in concentric circles, ripples
in an infinite pond reaching
all the way from my garden
to the outer rim of the galaxy,
with me at the center. Yeah
right, I'm a legend in my own

back yard, and when I'm gone,
it will still all be going on without me.

July 16 (dream poem)

I am travelling in a car with
my recently deceased friend Bill,
who is at the wheel, very much
alive and driving slowly.
We are rolling along a little
country road, a Hornby Island
kind of road, lined with dark trees.
We pass through a soft rain shower
and emerge into a warm spring day.
Suddenly, Bill points up, looking
out the window, drawing my attention
to the mountains, which I can see
if I duck down a little.

They are quite close, really,
huge, magnificent, rising steeply,
snow-capped, with wreaths of mist
around the peaks. Standing beside
the car, we become aware that there
is magic in the atmosphere.
Everything is so clear; with eagle vision,
we can see the treeline up incredibly high,
and above that, a single stone spire soaring
into the sky.

The scene shifts ... now I am driving back
the way we came. It is an older car, late 40's,
early 50's, a Chevy or a Buick, something
like that, and we are gliding along in a relaxed
and comfortable way. Bill puts his big hand
on my shoulder and thanks me for not being
in a hurry, taking it easy on the car, and just
generally taking it easy. The road wanders
past yellow fields and old farmhouses,
and even though I don't know where
we're going, it all feels wonderfully familiar.

July 17

I've noticed I'm not too interested
in making new friends anymore.
The old ones I've got suit me very well.
How many friends can one man have,
close friends and true? Four or three?
Maybe three or two? Close friends
I mean, and true. Even I, a relative recluse,
can claim a legion of acquaintances,
more than enough, if they all showed up,
for a fair-sized party at Government House.
But you know how I feel about parties.
I don't do them any more. I'd rather
spend the night at home, one on one
with my better half, or two on two
with some close friends and true.
Or alone.

July 18

A perfect summer day
for lunch in the country.
White linen, old silver,
French wine and bread.
Surrounded by a bower
of roses with a light wind
off the ocean, we are held
in a crystal bowl of refracted
light and colour, safe from
the darkness for a time.
Inevitably, Michael's death
comes up, and behind our sunglasses,
all three of us cry: my wife and I,
and our friend who loved him
and held him when he died.
A hush settles over the restaurant
rose garden for a moment,
like a swatch of impossibly sheer,
almost imperceptible fabric,
falling from the sky. In that moment,
I feel Michael passing by, and out of
the corner of my mind's eye,
I catch a glimpse of something;
maybe I am just imagining it.
But my wife and friend feel it too.
We can tell just by looking at each other.

July 19

My friend has lost his keys.
On the hot city sidewalk
we are worrying together.

July 20

Summer evening ...
it's no trivial matter
being human.

July 21

I sit beside the pond
carrying my woes,
and look ...
carrying the moon.

July 22

Rose petals fall ...
the wind drops
a door slams
then one more petal.

July 23

"What is the point
of meditating
if there is no point?"
I ask the roshi.
"That is the point,"
he replies.
"You are not trying
to accomplish anything"

Life itself is a koan.
You either get it
or you don't.
Sometimes I both
do and don't
in the same moment.

July 24

I clap my hands …
an explosion of birds
from the apple tree.

July 25

Eight year-old grandson
visiting for a few days.
Again, I understand why
the Creator decided
that only young people
should have children.

July 26

Both doors open
front and back.
Like a river,
the wind flows
through my house.

July 27

Small and green
they lie forlorn
on the lawn ...
apples fallen early
from the tree.

July 28

Remnants of a light
summer snowfall
caught me in the
barber's chair.
I brush away a few snippets
of white and silver hair
from the shoulders of
my dark blue shirt.

July 29

I scooped up the sun
in my bucket
and spilled it
glittering
on the grass.

July 30

Peacocks screaming
in the park, as though
it had suddenly occurred
to them that life is short.

July 31

Just about now I am
beginning to get tired
of the heat. That seems
to be the way of it, with
these hot days, the kind
I dream about deep
in the depths of winter.

Blue skies. Long evenings.
Green lawns. Bright mornings.
Open windows. I never get
enough ... I'm a creature
of the temperate zone, happiest
somewhere in the mid-70's,
Fahrenheit, Mr. West Coast
Vancouver Island, born and
born again. Now here comes
August, and as much as I hate
to say it, I am beginning to
get tired of the heat.

August 1

Face it sport, the little details of
your life are not always all that
interesting, and could easily be
consigned to the flotsam of the day.
Stop bothering us with the facts;
let's get down to the truth.
And for heaven's sake, let's make
room for illusions and fantasies,
the life of the unconscious.
This is our wild forest, complete
with its own valley of the shadow
where at night we experience
adventures to rival those of Ulysses,
returning in the morning to our safe
and sunny rooms.

August 2

slight breeze ...
ripples on the pond
rouse me from my
summer reverie.

August 3

Lying on a blanket
on the back lawn listening
to the radio close by my ear
watching birds in the apple tree
stretching breathing talking to myself
clouds are far below me as I lie on my
back looking down into endless space
it's eerie thinking I might fall and fall
forever but all I need to do is close
my eyes and return to the safe
darkness of myself lying on
a blanket on the back lawn
with the hot sun dancing
through the leaves.

August 4

A favourite nephew is married,
my sister's youngest son.
Many of us, mellowing about
her flower-splashed garden,

have never met before, but
we come together, strangers
in the brilliant sunshine,
to witness the beginning
of another chapter in
the rambling family novel.
Familiar words, food and drink,
eloquent toasts from surprising
people, laughter and fresh tears,
cameras, candles and cake.
As darkness falls the ritual
unfolds under a nearly full moon.
An auspicious occasion!
The destiny of the family
is enhanced!

August 5

To wake up,
try walking along
this wave-swept beach,
sandals in one hand,
cold water swirling
round your feet.

August 6

Sudden rain showers
falling on people
and flowers
indiscriminately.

August 7

Downtown
young amazons
in short skirts
striding into the wind.

August 8

Crowded sidewalk ...
with his dog
and begging bowl
the young addict sleeps
outside the coffee shop.

August 9

Down the street
a little girl is playing
her harmonica.
Suddenly, the afternoon
is transformed.

August 10

Darkness falls ...
brilliant red and green
fountains leap silently
into the sky ... then
the distant sound of fireworks.

August 11

While I am arranging a bouquet
of sweet peas over the kitchen sink,
one luminous violet blossom falls
at the feet of the little brass Buddha
seated on the windowsill.

August 12

Who can see the wind?
It's an old Canadian question,
most often asked on the prairies
when the sea of wheat sweeps
in waves toward the stark horizon.
Or in the deep evergreens where
the old growth sways like kelp
in an autumn storm. Or in my
back yard, where the filigreed
leaves of the Persian silk tree
dance like fish in the currents
of the tidepool afternoon.

August 13

Even the moon
looks a little tired
tonight we said,
leaving the party early.

August 14

My watering can,
half-full, half empty,
holds the evening sky.

August 15

Brushing an insect
from my hair,
a blossom falls instead.

August 16

My friend is avoiding me;
I don't want to see him either.
This is as it should be.

August 17

In the heat and hurly-burly
of the market, a young boy
steals a grape.

August 18

Should I grow a beard
and surrender to my age?
Should I be like Richard?
Big, shaggy and gray,
good for nothing but telling
people about themselves.

August 19

Your time is almost up Leo.
Yes, believe it or not, you may be
asked to swallow your pride and
give in to someone else's will.
Difficult for you, but concentrate
on acceptance and alleviate your
frustration by going for a long walk.
Don't worry; you will receive
some welcome news tomorrow,
as we move toward the orbit
of Virgo. This will help you
calm down. Visit with friends tonight.
Eat, drink, talk, laugh, man, woman.
All that stuff you do so well.
As for you Virgo, consider dropping
everything and meditating for an hour.
Stop drawing up plans and strategies.
Tell anyone seeking your opinion
that you need time to think about it.
Your key word for today is Zen!

August 20 *(at the lake)*

From the tangle by the beach,
my wife brings me four wild
blackberries to eat: the first
one sweet; the next two tart;
the last one fat, juicy and black,

very sweet indeed, so much so
I am disconcerted, in a delicious
sort of way, and feel compelled
to write myself a poem.

August 21

Water bomber
thundering, frightening
a solitary duck.

August 22

Beyond the mountains
a forest fire sunset.
On the dinner table
a single white rose.

August 23

Do I hear voices in the
treetops high above me?
Ravens in a talking circle.

August 24

Lying on my back
in rippling river,
eyes closed against
brilliant sun ...
eagle's shadow
falls across my face.

August 25

Petroglyph afternoon
squatting on warm black rock
at river's edge, hunting
for signs of prehistoric game.

August 26

On the cusp of another September,
I am busy with my broom, watching
the ground, watching the sky, saying
goodbye to my father the sun
and hello to my sister the moon.

August 27

A lot of little things.
Some work. Some bills.
Some errands. More work.
Following the list, buzzing
across town in my dusty
old car. My money flutters
away, released from its
tiny cage at the bank.
Flimsy paper bird, it flies
around squeaking, landing
on indifferent desks, to be
stamped into history.

August 28

Late summer is brown;
that's what it is when you
get right down to it.
Don't tell me about purple
and gold; brown is what's

happening in this late middle-
age time of the year.
Like the mottled skin
on an old jock's arm,
it's been too long in the sun.

August 29

The obese woman
across the street
screams at her husband
as he roars away
in his pickup truck.

August 30

Rebuilding the old house ...
carpenters hammering,
sawing, shouting, playing
the radio too loud!

August 31

Late at night
under a pale moon
my neighbour's dog
barks for an hour.

September 1

Another safari across the great water
in the bowels of the metal monster.
Then, we are released onto the highways
like greyhounds after a rabbit, rushing
out across the colossal grid of the city.
Two hours and two bad hamburgers later
we arrive like refugees from a stockcar
rally at the door to my daughter's house,
stunned, hot and tired, clutching our bags,
dying for a cup of tea.

September 2

*"Is it me the raven calls
from the world of shadows
this frosty morning?"*

*(Shukabo — died 1775 — from
"Japanese Death Poems")*

Michael did not have an opportunity
to write his own death poem. So we
write one for him on this summer afternoon.
Songs and stories, poetry and dance, tears
and laughter, food and drink and more tears,
not just for Michael but for Leslie too,
and for ourselves, reminded once again,
and again, as we grow older,
of our own mortality.

How many of us will write a farewell poem
before we set out on our final pilgrimage?
Here's mine:

Surely there's a river
on the road to paradise
where I can stop and skip
just one last stone.

(Three poems for Mary Helen)

September 3

An artist sketching?
A botanist collecting?
An architect designing?
A priestess conjuring?
A doctor seeking cures?
Yes ... it's Mary Helen, making
a map of this year's garden
to help us remember where
things will be growing
in the spring.

September 4

On the path of desire
one koan has my
full attention ...
you.

September 5

I am a loner.
I am a curmudgeon.
I am an introvert.
I am a child.
I am a complainer.
I am a windbag.

I am a bore.
Still, she seems to
love me even more
year after year.
Who can explain this?
Not me.

September 6

Elegant calligraphy ...
gnarled branches
of the oak tree
black against
the orange sunset.

September 7

Fierce little gargoyle
behind the white geranium,
protecting yard and garden
from intruders.

September 8

In the galaxy of my garden
three giant dahlias
glow like golden suns.

September 9

Late summer evening,
the light is fading fast.
At last the carpenters
up the street have downed
hammers and gone home.
Dogs and children will be
called inside sometime soon,
and traffic will settle for
the night. Then I'll go
outside again and listen
to the silence of the moon.

September 10

I notice I have been
writing about the moon
a lot lately. Reading
too much of the haiku
heroes of old Japan,
I guess, Basho, Issa,
Shiki and Buson.

But why not write about
the moon? Rather than
all the old stale stuff:
the morning blahs
the midnight blues
the tired baggage
hollow ambitions

empty promises
expectations unfulfilled.
Let's write about
the moon instead.

September 11

The smell of September:
orange peels and running shoes,
emanating from the old brick
schoolhouse a couple of blocks
away. September is the real
month of beginnings in this big
Canadian neck of the woods.
Holidays are over, summer is
packing up and heading south,
and it's back to work we go.

I remember the thrill of it all as a kid;
the lunchbox, the new shoes, the new jacket,
the new teacher ... and who's in your class
this year? (oh my god, it's Bubbles McRae!)
And the shiny, beautiful new set of pencil
crayons, the fabulous perfect rainbow of
luscious colours, some just so intoxicatingly
exotic, almost erotic in their tropical hues,
colours I could taste and smell and see
in dreams of treasure island, the emerald city
and the big rock candy mountain.

September 12

Another hectic day spins by
and finally I seat myself in
my favourite spot outside,
preparing to write a poem.
I wait a long time for my mind
to settle; I am tired and uninspired.
A tiny spider, suspended from
an invisible thread attached
to a branch of the oak towering
overhead, rappels through space,
lands on my empty page,
and scuttles away.

I sit for a few more minutes
waiting for words, and suddenly
bird shit fired from on high splats
on the bench about a foot from
my thigh, too close for comfort.

Eventually, I put pen to paper and
begin to write the first few lines
when my mother appears out of the blue,
red-faced and squinting, and hollers
"halloo, where are you?" Then she
spots me. "Oh there you are!" she says.
"I sure could use a cup of tea."
So on we go …

September 13

Sitting, thinking, watching
the thoughts drift by like
leaves in a quiet river,
floating slowly on the surface,
spinning in circles in back eddies,
sinking beneath dark fallen trees,
eventually disappearing downstream.
Sitting, not thinking, the thoughts
continue to flow by like leaves
in a river, whether I'm paying
attention or not.

September 14

Sitting outside
trying to write a poem
feel thick as a brick
can't get going
I musta been out here
an hour or more
bare feet on the grass
a little cool breeze
nice blue sky
neighbours winding down
flowers getting tired
but still beautiful
finally I throw in the towel
pack it in wind it up
wind it down close the book

on this baby and shut up shop
for the day. I go in the house
tell the wife how stupid I feel
she says there's your poem
and I say ok and write it down.

September 15

Home sweet home,
where heaven and earth,
desire and domesticity,
share the sacred space
between the dishwasher
and the stove.

September 16

Late summer evening
at Surreal Beach ...
for a moment another planet.

September 17

Wave on the beach,
bird in flight,
leaf on the water.
Each day different,
every day the same.

September 18

Sunset ...
nothing special ...
pearl mother
silver sister
golden father
brother jade.

September 19
(at a memoir-writing workshop)

Pens scratching,
long deep sighs,
flute playing
in quiet space.
The invisible
cloak of privacy
enfolds each person
descending deep
into the sacred
well of memory.

September 20

The first night of autumn ...
The solar-powered lantern
in my little garden temple
glows like a beacon in the
dark. All through the night
a solitary moth waits beside
the light. In the morning,
with the sunrise, it is gone.

September 21

In reflecting on the day
and what went down,
my mind wanders back
along the road to town
to the bank, the coffee shop,
the bookstore, the market,
the bakery and the football
field where I ran and jumped
and stood stock still.

But what I remember best
is the bouquet of dahlias
I picked and brought into
the house, a starburst of
rich late summer colours
for a gray and rainy
early autumn day.

September 22
(after Federico Garcia Lorca)

My heart of cedar bark
is filled with raindrops,
fir cones, blackberries
and river stones. I will go
very far, farther than
this range of mountains,
farther than the forest
forever, farther than the
sea itself, to find the heart
of my childhood, steeped
in mystery, with its crown
of ferns, and bow and arrow
made of garden twine and wood.

September 23

One delicate dahlia petal
fell from the bouquet
on the kitchen table.
I am holding it
in my right hand,
pinched gently between
thumb and forefinger,
in the direct light of
the late afternoon sun,
and it is glowing, an organic
composition of neon butter
yellow and deep red-orange

applied with deft strokes of
the finest imaginable brush.
A miniature watercolor
on a tiny piece of silk,
about the size of a human
eye, it is almost perfectly
elliptical, but not quite
perfect, which makes it
even more beautiful
than mere perfection.
I could go on; there is so much
more to say about this petal.
Really, I have only begun.

September 24

Two geese flying south …
my back yard
with its little pond
only a resting place.

September 25

Suddenly, a cold
autumn wind …
Why does that
ragged old beggar
look so surprised?

September 26

Wandering wasp,
nearing the end of a
hard season's labour,
escorted gently
from the house.

September 27

The ruins of Stonehenge,
my teeth. Lost another one
today to the endodontist.
Can you say "root canal
surgery?" Sure you can.
And, "the tooth is cracked;
it will have to come out."
But you're not smiling,
are you? So now I have
another hole in my head,
just what I need with
the winds of winter
right around the corner.

September 28

E-mail ... every day
more and more.
An ephemeral record
of communication
floating in from the ozone.
I even have messages from
friends who have died,
which I have saved for
months, and sometimes years.
I guess I'm not quite ready
to delete them ... forever.

September 29

Dark rain rides in from the west,
blooms and blows away.
The oak trees creak and sway
like sailing ships in a heavy swell.
A big soft fist of air knocks me
back a step or two and tells me
all I need to know about the wind.

September 30

Last day of September …
morning mist hangs
like a sheer white sheet.
A dream of people
on the street, fading in,
fading out.

October 1

Rising early, I'm half asleep,
with one foot dragging in the
dark dream river. From the
upstairs window I can see
the nearly-full moon sinking
in the west, immense and orange
in the golden dawn. I stagger
back to bed, but it's too late now.
I am awake and full of wonder

October 2

Pain …
always a messenger.
I call my dentist at home.
"Away for the weekend,"
his wife says.
"Take more pills."

October 3

Oak leaves falling in my yard,
more and more every day.
I can wait no longer.
Reluctantly, I take my rake
and go outside.

October 4

Waiting in the unseasonably
hot sun at the busy intersection
I am thrilled to find that I am
tucked in behind a city bus,
belching diesel fumes
(the bus, not me!).
Suddenly, across the way
I see a maple tree
all gold and yellow
with its leaves shivering
in the breeze and falling
gently to the ground.
For a moment, I see
nothing else; hours later
I see it still.

October 5

Musn't forget the gravy …
The gravy brings it all together.
The thought of hot, savoury
gravy on tender slabs of turkey
with spuds, mashed and steaming,
makes me pause to recall last night's
Thanksgiving dinner, in fragrant
delicious detail. The taste of earth,
the taste of heaven, with me in between.
So familiar. So necessary. So it goes,
year after year. At the oblong table,
my life, my people, motley and dear.

October 6

Not the greatest day,
I have to say.
Sunny and mild outside,
dark and cool inside.
I have no energy.
I have no humour.
I have no fun,
consequently.
"Much of life,"
Jung said, "is endurance."
I endured today.
And myself.
And it's ok.
Once in a while.

October 7

Reviewing my tiny financial empire
with my investment guy, I am struck
by how casually he talks about
what will happen when I die.
"Of course, this continues after your death,"
he says, smiling, nodding, tapping a page
of numbers with his pen, "and goes to
your wife." In the event that I die first,
my wife will be well taken care of.
If she dies first, I do not want to be
well taken care of. I want to be alone
for days at a time, to walk and sleep
and remember and dream, and heal,
if I live long enough.

October 8

Jagged candle flame …
the very breath
of autumn sighs
through the open window.

October 9

Morning fog
across the city.
Ghostly figures
appear and disappear

on the golf course.
Who plays golf
in the fog?
Could this be
an analogy for
the way most
of us behave?

October 10

A brisk walk in the scotch mist.
By the time we are half-way home,
it has turned to rain. We duck
under the lee of a sheltering tree
and continue our conversation.
So engrossed we are, we fail
to notice that the rain has stopped,
and there is enough blue in the sky
to "patch a Dutchman's pants,"
as my auntie Dinah used to say.

October 11

I must find a way
to keep my dreams
from scattering like
leaves in the cold
autumn wind.

October 12

Who is that stiff guy?
I ask myself, looking
at my reflection in the
store window as I am
strolling along the sidewalk.
He walks like a stick man,
I think, about as flexible
as a board. Better do
something about those
locked-up hips, buster;
good thing I'm on my way
to get a massage, a pain
in the ass, and I need it.

October 13

A long overdue hair cut.
The gentle soft woman who
lowers my ears lays me back
in her big old chair, washes
my hair in soapy warm water,
massages my skull, and with
soothing words murmurs in
her little intimate customer
voice, meant for my ears only,
about how she is doing now
that she has sold her condo.
I am half asleep under the
humming lights, with tropical
air blowing from the dryer,
and I am smiling, imagining
standing on some blue and
white beach with the wind
from the ocean just a little
too warm, buffeting me
with exquisite gusts.

Time to go; gently, I am
stood up and brushed off.
Handing over my money,
half-awake now, I sashay out
onto the late morning street.
The wind is cool and the clouds
are gray. All the way to my car,
I am as warm as a cat in a hat
by the fire, and as cute as a bug

in a rug. Once in the traffic, however,
I am back to the forbidding shores
of the Pacific Northwest. And my
reflection in the car mirror shows
that, although my head is now
smaller, my face is too big.

October 14

After much indecision,
I hung the golden earring
of the harvest moon
on the lowest branch
of the apple tree.

October 15

Cross-legged on the floor,
I watch the golden rush
of maple leaves pouring
through the air, blown
by the cold north wind.
The wind also carries the sea
and the mountains, blue and
white across the strait, and
the hint of a new ice age.
In my house, I am warm and silent.
Music for a zen garden plays softly:
first the koto, then the flute, then
the moment between the notes.

Outside, the wind has dropped.
The leaves are waiting for the next
gust, vibrating with anticipation.

October 16

Ikkyu Sojun (1394-1481)

*"The autumn breeze
of a single night of love
is better than a hundred
thousand years of sterile
sitting meditation."*

… mmm hmm …

October 17

Chuang-tzu (369-286 B.C.)

*"I dreamed I was a butterfly
dreaming I was a man."*

I dreamed I was a traveler
far across the sea on some
tropic isle, in some exotic city,
worried about airline schedules,
missing ferries, dragging
heavy luggage.

I remember calling home from
Thailand, from the tiny island of
Koh Samui, a long way out in the
Gulf of Siam, and talking to my
wife and daughter on the far side
of the world, crying like a fool
on the phone.

October 18

I can't be anyone
but me. I can't be
anywhere but here.
And even though I
often think of yesterday
and tomorrow, this very
moment is where my

life takes place; if I
miss this moment, I
miss my life.

October 19

Storm ... leaves race
along the street
and down the hill.

October 20

Sadly, we cut down
the dying apple tree.
Now, at least, we can
see more sky.

October 21

Every night at this time,
just at sunset, the ducks
are landing at the reservoir.
One by one; two by two,
in groups of three, five and seven,
they come soaring, circling
swiftly, landing with fabulous
confidence and grace, gently
on the glowing water.

Clucking contentedly,
they paddle in circles all
together, home and dry.

October 22

on the back steps
gumboots full
of rain.

October 23

I just paid three-fifty for a coffee,
served in a cardboard cup.
I remember paying ten cents for
a cuppa coffee at Woodward's
lunch counter, in the basement
of the old store, up at the top
of Third Avenue, back in the old
home town, served in a heavy
white crockery cup, with a lip
as thick as a bicycle tire, and
a saucer to catch the drips.
God, how I loved that stuff,
along with a freshly-made
brown sugar doughnut, warm
from the doughnut machine.
Mind you, the coffee was
pretty plain, not your grande
mocha toffee-nut easy whip
extra hot latte, just your basic

Juan Valdez, percolated in what
looked like a small cement mixer
next to the grill by the kitchen door.
When was that? In another lifetime,
perhaps, when I was fifteen. Why,
back then, a cup of coffee cost
a thirty-fifth of what it costs now.
And I actually had to walk five miles
to school and back, sometimes,
through two or three feet of snow.

October 24

In the Japanese garden
I am searching for
the perfect photograph,
satori on a strip of film.
The little maple tree,
red leaves ignited
by the afternoon sun,
is so compelling
I fail to notice that
I too am aflame.

October 25

Do the laundry.
Rake the leaves.
Sweep the sidewalk.
Pick the last
of the flowers
for a bouquet.
Stop at the bakery.
Gas up the car
and check the oil.
Feed the birds.
Vacuum the hall.
Visit my mother.
Stop at the bank
for some cash
(my father was
a cash guy; so am I).
Park downtown,
pick up some photos,
grab a quick coffee,
run down to the book
store and the music
store, buy gifts for
birthdays, bustle home
in the traffic, check
the answering machine
and the e-mail, turn up
the heat, lie down for
a while, sleep a little,
think about dinner,
carry water, chop wood,
wash my bowl.

October 26

In the produce
department the young
clerk furtively fondles
the kiwi fruit.

October 27

The little dog tied
outside the market
barks fiercely at
shoppers going in,
but not at shoppers
coming out.

October 28

Exhausted, the young
cashier cheerfully says,
"How are you?" as I finally
reach the front of the line.
"Oh, fine thanks," I say,
frazzled, hot and bothered,
"and how are you?"
"Great!" she responds,
manhandling the potatoes
and the cat food into
a plastic bag.

October 29

On this dank and dreary day,
memories of childhood come
seeping back, faded snapshots
of standing at the window, sad,
restless and tired, watching
rain run down the glass.

October 30

Sunny Day, wearing
a white Stetson, rides
in from the west
on a fresh horse and
blows the big bad
Cloud Brothers,
ominous in their long
black coats, away.

October 31

A windy brilliant afternoon...
I am taking my mother to the bank
to help her with her dollars and
declining sense of competence
in the face of the mundane world.
It is sobering, even saddening,
to see her fumbling with her papers,
telling irrelevant stories to the

nice young man who is patient,
distant and polite. This woman,
who was once so courageous
and in control fifty years ago,
now struggles to stay afloat
in the stream of everyday life.
Daughter, sister, mother, wife,
now great-grandmother, she is
within hailing distance of extreme
old age, and she is afraid.

November 1

Rain rattling on the roof,
running in rivulets along the road.
The warm Pacific wind is as sweet
and heavy as pineapple juice.
November blows in right on cue,
clearing the decks for winter.

Note:

The memories for the following series of
poems — November 2 to 17 - were triggered
by the smell of tobacco, which still clung to some
family artifacts I recently inherited. Most of the
men in my family smoked — and the heaviest
smoker of them all was my Uncle Fred (as we
called him), about whom I have written the first
poem in the series.

November 2

He wasn't really my Uncle Fred,
but we called him that anyway.
A life-long bachelor, he was
definitely into all that traditional
macho stuff from the 30's and 40's:
smoking, whisky, cards, hunting,
laughing at women. And fly fishing,
about which there is so much more to say.

Fred was a butcher by trade.
Down in my uncle Ted's grocery
store he chopped through joints
of meat with his black-handled
cleaver, blood on his apron, guts,
bones and pig's knuckles on the
sawdust floor. He let me drive the old
green '48 Dodge delivery truck, even
before I had a license, and managed
to refrain from hitting me when I
buggered the clutch, although
his face twisted and his fingers
twitched. "Jesus Christ!" was all
he said, through his teeth, furiously
lighting up another cigarette. Chain
smoking, that's what they called it,
and I knew that if he could have,
he would have smoked chains too,
leaving a smudge of rust in the
ashtray overflowing with iron butts.
My uncle Fred coughed himself to death.

Despite the admonitions of Dr. Chisholm,
his drinking buddy and poker crony,
a smoker himself who favoured a pipe,
Fred continued to smoke right to the day
my father took him away to the hospital
in the '48 Dodge delivery truck.

In his room upstairs in my aunt's big house,
he left several graceful, elegant, well-worn
bamboo fishing rods, with the tools and
delicate clutter required for the tying
of flies, tiny exquisite creations, irresistible
to river trout, which he created like a jeweler
for fish; flies with exotic, mysterious names:
Silver Doctor, Royal Coachman, Dark Montreal,
Parmachene Belle, and his favourite, the old
Mickey Finn. "Keep your lines tight and
your threads smooth," he would say with a grin,
"and never leave home without Mickey Finn."

November 3

Opening credits: letters in white,
Brighton Light Italic, perhaps, or
Eros Demi-Bold, appearing and fading
onscreen, while the camera, slowly pans
along the immense silver-gray expanse
of Long Beach, on the west coast
of Vancouver Island. The surf roars;
in the distance, the long white breakers
surge toward the beach. Rainforest snags

stand stark against the sky, black relief
above the impenetrable green wall
of old growth. Inland, the mountains
lean crazily, jagged, shrouded with clouds;
humps and loaves and blue volcanoes.
The air is filled with mist; the filtered sun
glistens on the heaving mercury sea,
huge waves burst against the rocks
around the small island far offshore.
It looks like a stranded battleship;
in effortless slow motion, the explosions
of spray leap skyward.
Born in the rainforest, I was frightened
by the ocean (oh those childhood dreams
of huge black swells looming over my
fragile boat).

November 4

This is small town stuff, for the most part:
sawmill smells, fishing boats, green fields
and rivers. And the forests everywhere
and all around, jungle and refuge, haunted
by the ghosts of dead Indians and wounded
loggers. Silent predators lurk along the
overgrown trails that cut through the trees;
the walk home from school features a running
gun fight every day – eerie shapes in the shade
nick in behind the telephone pole - zap!
I pick them off one by one as I bob and
weave my way along the dirt path beside

Beaver Creek Road; hulking creatures move
like the shadows of clouds, behind the trees,
behind the swamp, behind me, and I run
until my chest burns, until I burst out into
the light, out from under the smothering damp
stale clinging skunk cabbage canopy of trees.

November 5

Walking home alone after a movie at the Roxy Theatre
- Abbott and Costello Meet Frankenstein, I think —
the wind in the swaying trees makes that fearsome
low sound — whooooo — conjuring bulgy-eyed
murderers who spring, knife blades gleaming,
from behind the clumps of long grass that shudder
by the side of the road. Don't turn around!
And if you do, move slowly, carefully, with
confidence and poise, glancing over your shoulder
as casually as you would at a distant stranger.
And if you see the slight shift in space, the invisible
darting shadow that snaps behind the hedge, turn back
slowly, flip your imaginary cigarette away, walk on
at a relaxed medium speed, and don't show the whites
of your eyes! If they see that ... swoosh ... they've
got you; they rip out your throat and scream with glee
as your blood trickles across the highway and you kick
yourself to death sucking for air that never comes.

November 6

The Alberni Valley, forty miles from the sea,
at the head of the long dark fjord, where the
Somass River meets the salt chuck, where the
rain starts in November and sometimes doesn't
stop until May. Father ... log-boom dancer,
high rigger, climbs a tall straight fir, faller's
spurs biting deep into the bark, double-bitted axe
swinging by his side. A hundred feet up, he chops
off the top of the tree; it falls roaring through the air,
smashing to the forest floor. A ragged cheer rises
from the crew. Sitting on the swaying spar, he rolls
and smokes a cigarette, then stands, hands on his hips,
and gazes down the mountainside, Il Duce of the
old growth kingdom. In this faded family photo,
there he is, up there, part daredevil, part god,
half in love with death, while on the ground,
his six-year old son looks up in awe and trepidation.

November 7

Just outside my back door
and down the old gravel road,
I remember running then diving
headlong into the swimming hole
at Kitsuksis Creek (those Indian words
were a mouthful) mashing my face
into the muck on the bottom. I would
make rafts from floating wood and old
boards, and bobble along the creek for

hours, inevitably falling in, thrashing
to shore, trudging home filthy,
sodden and satisfied.

One hot and silent summer day, I climbed
out on the branch of a giant maple overhanging
a stretch of the stream, marsupial boy in the trees,
where the forest closed in like a canopy of huge,
luminous umbrellas; the water was murmuring,
green and clear; the dappled sunlight played on
the rocks on the bottom, all mottled and white.
Caught in a crystal fish bowl, I was suffused
with joy, embraced by the light and the heat.
Radiant unconscious gratitude to the gods
of summer and trees and life soared through me
and out into the world, and like a bowl, I was open
to receive whatever was offered from above.

November 8

Flashback to Ucluelet, 1953 ("that's U-Clue-Let, you oaf,
not U-Kew-Let"), a fishing village, fifteen miles south
of Long Beach, where twice a week, the *Uchuk*, the small
freighter and ferry, arrived from Port Alberni, laden with
supplies, newspapers, fuel, and a homegrown gaggle
of fishermen, loggers, friends, relatives, and there ...
covering his ears against the blast of the whistle, a tall
skinny twelve-year old boy with glasses, clutching
a suitcase filled with clean clothes, carefully packed
by his mother.

"McGee! McGee!" It was cousin Paddy, running
down the dock, two years older, also thin as shiplap,
with big ears and soft lank hair. Together, the two boys
walked up the hill to the big old house where Auntie Jo
and Uncle Bill and cousins Ellen and Mike lived. But first,
a stop at the swing hanging from a branch on the arbutus tree
that stooped out over a tangle of blackberry vines, the beach
below awash in the oily water of the bay. They each took
a turn, running, launching, sailing out over the cliff's edge,
and back again to the base of the tree. Then on up to
the house, spacious, gothic and friendly, except during
the wild storms of winter when the winds from the
open Pacific swept across the harbour and slammed
into the aging wooden structure, which groaned
and shuddered, all the windows rattling in a different key.
Paddy and McGee would take turns playing spooky tunes
on the piano, while the other crept up the long narrow
flight of stairs, quaking with each creak, while all around
the storm boomed and roared in its inchoate way,
leaves and branches whirling through the salty air.

November 9

When the wind dropped briefly the boys could hear
the winter surf on the rocks at Big Beach a mile away,
a battery of immense distant cannons shaking the earth
with its deep concussions. McGee felt the tremors right
through his boots, and reluctantly followed Paddy
along the sodden forest trail to a vantage point high
in the swaying trees above the beach. Colossal gray
and black waves smashed over boulders as big as houses,

tossing clusters of battered logs, some weighing several tons,
high in the air, then rushed up the beach toward the cliff,
over the pools and puddles and heaps of broken kelp,
right up into the fringe of the forest, sucking at the
exposed roots of the cedar trees that would soon fall
before the onslaught. The beach was a terrifying
panorama of wild activity, everything aswirl and
heaving; the air full of driven cold spray, the roar
of the waves a continuous subterranean thunder.

November 10

Many years later, McGee would dream
of running from the police down onto
a long sandy point jutting into the sea.
The police moved in slowly, from several
directions, confident of catching their man
as he dodged helplessly about among the
scattered trees. Finally, he was cornered
and surrendered meekly. As they left
the beach and trudged up into the forest,
the policemen and McGee suddenly felt
compelled to turn and look back at the sea.
Huge, ominous waves were rolling in,
biting off and swallowing chunks of beach,
moving swiftly and inexorably toward
the suddenly panic-stricken party, poised
on the very edge of oblivion. They all ran
desperately for higher ground as the great
waves destroyed beach and trees behind them.

Then the dream shifted, the camera held
a long, lingering shot from high above
a tiny island far at sea. The waves swiftly
covered the island and washed it away in
a matter of minutes. We can see it down there,
disappearing under the cold blue water, and on
all sides, the dark ocean, streaked with foam,
stretches away to the horizon.

November 11

… well, Paddy and I had Long Beach
all to ourselves for several golden summers.
With our 22's, we would shoot at the green
glass fishing buoys that floated in on the tide
from Japan. Entire afternoons passed, and
we saw no one, hiking for miles along the hard,
gray sand to the "dunes," where we gathered
strands of cordite, left from practice bombing
runs for the big war just ten years before.

We stuffed the cordite into empty steel
shell casings we would sometimes find,
then light the home-made fuse. The shell
would hiss, roar, shoot flames and tumble
across the dunes in crazy jagged patterns.
When Uncle Bill found out what we were doing,
he got all heavy and told us we could have been
killed, blown to bits, 'cause cordite is what bombs
are filled with, and he ordered the dunes off-limits.

November 12

Years later, I worked for the logging company survey crew
during the summers of high school and university, and helped
lay out the road from the Alberni Valley to Long Beach,
up the switchbacks, snaking across the mountainsides,
along the Taylor River, over the pass, the dust sifting
through the floorboards of the "crummy." Then out into
the soft light of early morning, axes, compass and chain
in hand, and off up the hill, past the bulldozer, poised like
a steel dinosaur in the fallen trees, and into the forest for
a day of climbing and measuring, swatting mosquitos,
and fighting angry yellow jackets. In the late sixties,
when the road was wide open, before the creation of
a national park, a sacred enclave, protected from barbarians,
I saw the beach crowded, crammed, a'crawl with campers.
Motorcycles and muscle cars spun across the sand, and once
I watched the smoldering hulk of a 1958 Oldsmobile,
abandoned in the surf, sink beneath the waves and disappear.

I couldn't go back for years after that, not even when I lived
only eighty miles away, and the road was perfect and paved.
To think that I once had the beach to myself, and nobody
seemed to care. I assumed, of course, it would always
be that way.

November 13

Basketball ... in the last few seconds of the game,
I was fouled and received two free throws. I was fourteen,
and we trailed those gnarly, pimply, threatening hard-ass
clods from Courtenay and Cumberland, surly buggers who
drank and smoked stogies. I hated their putrid green uniforms,
their logger's socks and black, clunky running shoes.
The Junior "A" Athletics, for whom I played, wore white
and gold uniforms with white runners, a lot classier,
I always felt. I hit the first free throw, and we were down
by one point. I hit the second and tied the score! Hurray!
It's overtime and we have another chance. What? I stepped
over the line. Free throw disallowed. We lost 49-48.
I ran down to the locker room, that dank cement cellar
in the old Alberni Athletic Hall, and cried.
Pounding away in my back yard, I flung up jump shots
from the corner by the garbage can, hook shots over
the clothes line, and long one-handers from out near
the apple tree. Down at the hall on Saturday night,
November, 1955, the Senior A's are beating the
detested heavies from Vancouver. The place is
packed to the sidelines, and there I am, slapping
up the wooden numbers, zealously guarding my
vaunted position at the scoreboard. Sipping a

Kik Cola, I study Carol-Ann Gaston's legs poking
out from under her plaid pleated skirt. The crowd
roars; a snake dance spontaneously erupts across
the court; the beer parlours will be bulging tonight.
Later, we share another Kik and I walk Carol-Ann
home, holding her hand, the first sweaty palm I can
recall, clutching my own in some kind of desperation.

November 14

The intense erotic business of being sixteen, lying on
the hot boards of the dock at the lake, my wet hair
just touching the feet of Carolyn Jones. Dark, svelte
Carolyn, brown as an otter, and just as elusive.
I felt like a clumsy bull in futile pursuit of a deer.
The wharf rocked gently in the afternoon waves,
hypnotic and surreal; the rhythm of the water passed
through the wood to the bodies burning on the boards.

Leslie was there, diving, slipping in and out of the water,
risks sparkling and splashing from her fingertips.
We went steady for two weeks, Leslie and I; danced
together to Blue Suede Shoes; kissed in the cold night air
at her front door. She hugged me, and I was surprised,
stiff and breathing like a horse. But the girls in my group
were too much for me, and, I discovered a lifetime later,
that they felt the same about me.

November 15

What can you say about your home town?
You can only choose a few representative
samples from the river of images.
Let's take a scoop here and a scoop there
and splash a few memories over the rocks.

Then ... and still ... it's the river and the lake.
Hunkering down, watching the endless green
tapestry of light flowing by, floating in the clear
water, face down, staring at the sunbeams
dancing silently over the white sand bottom.
Hot summer days at the lake, let's say
at the Berry's place, late July. The boys are
together for a swim, a laugh, and a few cold beer.
Down on the dock, there's Reg, Stick, Ken and
Daff; Yogurt and Weiner are up at the house,
playing pool on the porch. Elvis, Little Richard
and Fats are spinning on the box ... and so
it seemed it would be seamless summer forever,
with boat trips to the head of the arm, carousing
among the islands, leaping off cliffs, careening
around the trails, shrieking at the mountainside,
just to hear the echo, falling in the water fully-
dressed. Adolescence, wild and ecstatic,
unconscious and sad.

November 16

And work ... the mills and the logging shows high
in the hills offered plenty of jobs to able-bodied
high school cannon fodder willing to work in the noise
and the stink, to cope with the stupefying boredom
of feeding and cleaning huge filthy machines.
Needed the money, though ... My mother pulled
a small string; I was offered a job on the summer
survey crew, July, 1957. Three-fifty an hour,
not bad. Five summers, and for every serene
sweeping mountain valley and clean snow-fed
waterfall, with its sheets of cold mist sifting
over the bluffs and towering shoulders of trees,
there was a three-hour round trip in the back of
the rotten crummy, the company bus that came
around every morning to pick up the loggers
and the motley little survey crew, and deliver
us all to the morning forest, an hour and a half
away, over twenty-five miles of fractured
and dusty gravel roads.

The loggers in the crummy, loaded with beer
and sausage from the night before, and eggs
and coffee for breakfast, dozed, smoked, chewed
snuff, spat brown puddles on the wretched floor-
boards of the crummy, belched, farted, grumbled
and swilled more coffee from their thermoses.
We jounced along under the stars of "early shift"
(at work by four a.m. and out of the tinder-dry
woods by noon), jumped from the crummy,
stood gasping in the dust, then stumbled into the

bush to curl up somewhere for an hour's sleep.
Often, we would climb high into a mountain
meadow, following the compass and the chain,
counting the trees, and eat lunch gazing far
across the valley to higher peaks, still crowned
with snow. Sometimes, eagles would float down
from somewhere even higher up, spin their great
circles in the sky, then glide into the deep shadow
of a distant cliff, immense and looming,
like a mythic fortress.

November 17

My father loved the mountains around the Alberni Valley
as only a true wild child of nature can love something
so vast and beautiful. He climbed them all, with his
bum leg and back, gave names to peaks and rivers
and lakes, shot deer, drank whisky. Took pictures too,
black and white snapshots … and there they are,
Mom and Dad, up at Winnifred Lake (named after
my mother) beyond the head of Taylor Arm,
in behind Mount Klitsa. Mom with kerchief, shorts
and a big pack, Dad with another bulging pack,
caulked boots laced up high, grinning at the camera,
with his crooked teeth and Navajo nose.
Uncle Kelly and Aunt Lillian, in the background,
laughing, heads together, deep in one of their private jokes
which used to irritate my mother so.

"August is the time to go," Dad rasps. "Snow's all gone."
Shakes his head, lights another hand-rolled cigarette,

smiles his old raggedy-ass, jagged pirate smile, and says,
"Damn, those meadows in behind Klitsa , just like a park.
Lovely little lakes, all kinds of wildflowers, the most
spectacular country you'll ever see. Fred and I had
a hunting cabin back up on Dog Mountain. God!
I can remember packing a deer out of there, all the way
to the lake, then having to cut it up in chunks to get it all
in the boat. Whole area's probably logged off by now.
No more deer. Christ! It makes me so goddamn mad
to see mile after bloody mile of desolation.
Somebody should have put a stop to it all years ago."

November 18

Back in the present, I am ready
to return to myself, here and now.
I will revisit that familiar foreign
country of the past I know,
time and time again.

I'm as interested in where I came
from as where I am now, and where
I am going. In some essential way,
I see that I am as I was; I am as I am;
I am as I will be. But different.
Before enlightenment, trees are trees
and mountains are mountains.
You know how it goes.

November 19

The snow comes
as a surprise,
and we are children
for a while.
But the snow stays
too long, and we are
adults again.

November 20

Six months ago
the garden was perfect.
Now, under winter's
first snow, it is
perfect again.

November 21

She rises early
to go for a run
her warm scent
on the pillow.

November 22

Walking downstream ...
yellow leaves in
the current running
ahead of me.

November 23

Looking up
it's clear tonight
all the way
to Venus!

November 24

Cold snap!
Little pleasures of winter:
woolly gloves, warm hat,
two pairs of socks.

November 25

seed catalogue
in the mail ...
dreams of summer
dreams of spring

November 26

Guests for dinner ...
I have vaccumed the
hall carpet twice today
and now have to
do it again.

November 27

One man singing
to himself walking
in the night, frozen
breath disappearing
among the stars.

November 28

Heavy fog lifts.
Fortunately
I am not where
I thought I was.

November 29

Winter basement ...
a colony of spiders
in the old watering can.

November 30

Wood for the fireplace.
Thanks for this final service
to the snow-broken branch
fallen from the old oak tree.

December 1

Downtown the old wino
holds out his ragged
Santa Claus hat and
collects a few snowflakes.

December 2

Morning snow.
A tiny path
across the yard …
cats and raccoons.

December 3

Chopping wood
freezing wind …
then Scrabble
by the fire.

December 4
(trip to the massage therapist)

The hole in my back is black.
It's a black hole, alright, and
it feels like one. A black hole
burned into my back; black
from the charcoal and the
flames which have incinerated
my old wooden framework.
It's on the right side of my
superstructure, below my three
floating ribs, beside my spine,
deep in the tissue, down in my
foundation of bone and sinew.
I hurt myself I guess, standing
too close to the fire.

December 5

I bought a Christmas turkey today
and stashed it in the freezer. Today,
I spread out all the gifts I've purchased
to see if I have missed anything, looking
for an opportunity to buy some more.
Today my mind wandered back to the
balcony of my memory, far from the
screen and the teeming stage, to the day
we chose the Christmas tree with my aunt,
cut it down, and brought it back from
the farm in the sleigh, drawn by the old
horse Dolly. It took three men, including
my father, to haul the tree into the house
and stand it in the living room, next to
the grand piano. At the age of eleven,
I could only watch in awe and breathe
the cold fragrant air, a fresh heady tang
of evergreen, hard and sweet and clear.

December 6

An evening alone ...
basketball on tv
a second cup of tea
a mandarin orange
folding laundry
early to bed.
Perfect.

December 7

More Christmas shopping ...
socks and chocolate
for my nephews.
They don't need
either of these things.
But that is beside the point.

December 8

After the pristine snow,
the grubby world returns.
Dirt on the road, sodden
heaps of rotting leaves,
the once proud Frosty
in the school yard now
just a puddle of slush.

December 9

Last light pale orange
on the horizon.
Disciplined ducks
dash across the moon,
black brush strokes on
the fading tapestry of night.

December 10

Christmas decorations
springing up around my
neighborhood, ranging from
blazing panoplies of seasonal
archetypes to a few coloured
bangles at the gate.

I like Mrs. Crabtree's minimalist
approach: one modest wreath
with a tiny silver bell. As you can
probably tell, I haven't put my
lights up yet. I will, but not
very many, and only when
the time is right.

December 11

My sister bought an artificial
Christmas tree this year,
"complete with decorations,"
she said, "but I will miss
the smell of a real tree."

I bought a real tree today,
stuffed it in the trunk of the car,
drove it home in the wind and rain,
stood it up in a bucket of water
outside the basement, propped
against the house.

Already, you can pick up the scent
leaking under the back door: iced
spearmint coniferous salt water tea,
bittersweet and bracing, fresh from
the forest, cold and green. A real
tree it has to be, for the scent,
if for nothing else.

December 12

Winter storms chase each other
across the cringing landscape,
wild Nordic giants on the loose.
Vicious winds breaking trees,
smashing fragile plans and
expectations. On days like this,
the earth is vulnerable and small,
a little blue ball, falling through space.
Like the earth, I too am blue, falling
through life. What to do? Sit it out,
like always. And write a poem or two.

December 13

Ah, yes. This is the kind
of winter day I enjoy.
We're only a week
from the solstice, and
today I can see it coming
in the smooth gray dolphin's
fin of cloud sliding across
the ocean in the soft pearly
light of afternoon.

December 14

Christmas songs on the radio carry me
back to the day fifty-two years ago when
I stood outside my school, important in
my safety patrol uniform, at the crosswalk
on Beaver Creek Road, silent and alone
for a blessed while in the magical snowfall,
weeping delicious crocodile tears, singing
to myself, "I saw mommy kissing Santa Claus."

December 15

Coffee and cookies at my friend's house.
We exchange Christmas cards and complain
about the weather. She weeps bitter tears
over the death of her father last spring,
regrets her broken marriage, misses her

ex-lover, now living with his mother.
We agree that life is full of swell surprises,
and oh well, there is still a lot to look
forward to, and go on to talk about movies
and music and plans for the holidays.

December 16

Quiet Sunday morning.
The rain has stopped.
In the distance the sound
of cathedral bells.

December 17

Lunch downtown with the lads.
Thai, medium-hot. Eight men,
about four hundred and fifty years
old, altogether. With eleven or
twelve wives (historically speaking),
eight daughters, three sons, incredibly
diverse careers, money in the bank,
food in the fridge, two cars (one old),
travels ending or in the offing to Japan,
India, Nepal, all the Hawaiian Islands,
Ukraine, Morocco, Mexico and Peru.
Mothers dying, fathers dead, working
hard, thinking about retiring, trying
to stay ahead of the game.

December 18

First the star, then the lights,
followed by the wreaths, silver
and blue, and the sugar-frosted
balls and baubles. Finally, the tinsel
too is hung with care, and the lights
turned on. There! Isn't that beautiful?
Is it only a year since we last stood here
staring like children at the Milky Way?

December 19

The world will have me
as it wishes. I cherish
the illusion that I have
some control,

but I don't. I am a passenger
on a capricious planet who changes
her mind without consulting me.
And there is no "grand scheme
of things." It's just here and now,
yesterday, and the day after
tomorrow.

December 20

A big old Christmas stocking,
stuffed with the riches of life.
A safe warm haven from
the brutish winds of winter.
A small anthropological museum,
with treasures from the seven
corners of the world. A storehouse
of esoteric knowledge. A precious
egg of Castanadian energy protecting
the beating heart of the family.
My house.

December 21

Like wild animals, we lay in stores
against the future. The ancient patterns
of the prehistoric past kick in, and our
old hunter-gatherer selves go walkabout
at the market and the mall. Food, drink,
clothing, pile them on. Gather the clan,
take the lid off the pot, keep enough for
yourself and give the rest away.

December 22

A polished red ornament hangs
on the tree, turning with the light
and the heat; images reflect like
memories in the crystalline heart
of a ruby. In the world of the red
ornament, continents walk by
on their way to the kitchen, and
oceans flow from room to room.
In the background, an entire
civilization sits down to dine,
then drives home under a new moon.

December 23

"When I raised my head,"
wrote Seibi in 1852,
 "there was my rigid body
lying bitter cold."

In my warm bed this morning,
I felt once again the bleak wintry
grip of despair, reviewed the blue
and gray outlook for the day,
and wished for something else.
Later, reading some haiku,
Seibi's death poem
drew me in immediately.

December 24

Six a.m. My winter face
in the bathroom mirror is
fish-belly white; there is luggage
under my eyes. I look my age
and then some. The house is cold.
I eat an orange and read the newspaper.
I feel old and tired. But my daughter
is coming for dinner tonight and the
weather is brightening up. Another
cup of tea, and I should be ready
for Christmas.

December 25

No big surprises this year,
but many small ones,
some quite exquisite,
like delicate Christmas
tree decorations, suspended
from the branches
of everyday life.

December 26

A day of nibbling at
Christmas leftovers.
Friends coming by
later this afternoon.
I'll retreat, read my
new novel and have
a little snooze; always
a good idea before
wine and conversation.
It's a tough life, I know.
Maybe that's why
it's not always fun.

December 27

A distant train whistle ...
like a streamliner, effortlessly
gliding along the tracks,
carries me back down
the long time line to the past,
to when I was nine, running
to the station, heart pounding,
to meet someone I loved.

December 28

Lunch alone in the
Japanese restaurant.
Looking out onto the busy
sun-streaked street, I drink
my tea, eat my sushi and soup,
and listen to the young man and
woman at the next table talking
on their cell phones.

December 29

Winter visit to the physio ...
Bend, twist and stretch
she tells me. "Pretty good
forward and backward,"
she says, "but not so good
sideways." How could she
know the story of my life?

December 30

The wind from the west
is raw and cold and sweet.
Well, maybe not sweet
in the usual sense ...
in the sense of waking up,
maybe, to the stark stunning
winter beauty of snowcapped
mountains and the dark blue sea.

December 31

We stay up late for us
and watch a movie.
Finally, at eleven or so,
my wife drifts off to bed,
and I crash in front of the
tube to watch the fireworks
around the world.
Soon, the neighborhood erupts
with screams and shouts;
music blares out briefly-open
doors and windows, drunken
buffoons bellow at the midnight
moon. I step out on the front porch
for a minute or two as the old year
clatters by like a broken stagecoach,
smiling to myself, looking back,
looking ahead, full of wonder,
with a tremor of despair,
ready for bed at last.

January 1

January first.
The faces of the
people on the
street in Chinatown
don't look any different
than they did last year.

January 2

Interviewing the artist for a
magazine profile, I am struck
by the depth of his obsessions,
so different from mine.
The daemon of creativity is
a promiscuous muse; she will
have us both in completely
different ways.

January 3

Already the days are
a few minutes longer.
Driving home in the late
afternoon, I see an opening
in the gray ocean of cloud,
a vast curtain unfolding
to reveal a celestial stage
of brilliant blue, and I

catch a glimpse of the sun
shining down on the magic
kingdom of my dreams.

January 4 *(dream poem)*

I met two different women
on my trip to the Yukon or
Alaska, or somewhere
in northern Canada.
The first, in the restaurant,
was Swedish, perhaps,
European for sure,
insouciant and smooth
in a fur-lined jacket with
a Bergmanesque style, warm
and cool simultaneously,
delicious to pursue.

The second, in the front seat
of the truck, was a successful
frontier entrepreneur, running
her own newspaper in this isolated
oil or diamond town in the northwest
territories. Her jacket smelled of
wood fire; she had a strong nose
and a forest of curly hair.

The first laughed and suggested
that I come back again, perhaps,
sometime soon. The second

kissed me in the front seat
of the truck, but ever so adroitly
deflected my intention.

These anima beauties of mine;
they do want to keep me on
the straight and narrow.

January 5

(Poem for Peter)

Crying in the bathroom
this morning, I don't want
to think about Peter, but
I cannot help myself.

It's too early yet
to write this poem.

We remember the windstorms
he created, making his own
weather as he blew through life.
His departure brought us all
together, like travellers around
the fire at night, heading west
through the high mountain passes.

January 6

Gas up the car.
Return the too-small
Christmas slippers
for a larger pair.
Buy some stamps.
Pay some bills.
Go for a walk
in the cold wind.
Do some yoga.
Vacuum the hall,
clean the bathroom,
write some poetry,
prepare dinner,
wash the dishes,
get ready for bed.
Nothing is really
more important than
anything else, from a
zen point of view.
Except maybe the slippers.

January 7

Snowfall ...
the north side
of the oak trees
dressed in sheer
white lingerie.

January 8

stone labyrinth
in our garden
suggested
under the snow.

January 9

West coast car doors
all frozen shut.
Manitoba morning
caught us with our
long johns down.

January 10

After walking safely
to the grocery store,
I slip and fall
in my own driveway.

January 11

A brief moment
in the sun, sheltered
from the wind ...
heaven sent.

January 12

The waning moon
shrinks brilliantly
in the cold black night.

January 13

Folding laundry
warm from the dryer...
heavy woollen mitts
still a little damp.

January 14

An ever-so-light
dusting of snow ...
it fell before dawn,
in the last minutes
of dream time,
and like my dream,
was gone before noon.

January 15

I'm doing the jock potato thing,
watching young black and white
millionaires run up and down
the field or the court, flying
through the air, crashing to
the ground or the floor,
gesticulating to the raving
fans and the chorus line of
air-brushed cheerleaders,
dancing on the edge
of anonymity.

Suddenly, I feel old and sad.
Those are children out there
in the bodies of gods and
goddesses. They have so
much more to learn, and so
much yet to be broken.

January 16

My oldest friend quietly
tells me he has prostate
cancer. "Surgery in a month,"
he says. "The good news is
that it hasn't spread, it hasn't
spread." He says it twice, so
I know how he is feeling.

January 17

Why do I deliberately set myself up
to write another of these damn magazine
articles? Trying to tell a complex story
in a clear and simple way. That's all
there is to it! Yet I'm sweating rubber
bullets and shitting paper bricks and
waking up at the hour of the wolf
with my guts in a knot, obsessively
mixing metaphors. Stupid, I know.
I'll finish the friggin' article, and feel
so much better in the end, as I always do.
"Taurus is a slow learner,"
the astrologer tells me.

January 18

Eyes closed, sitting in the bleachers …
… sheltered from the wind …
… facing into the fragile sunshine …
… the sound of my breathing …
. . .dogs barking in the field …
… shouts from the soccer game …
… a distant airplane …

Now I have something
to write about.

January 19

When I was young, we would have called him
a "bum," this self-appointed superintendent
of our neighborhood park and field. With his
massive pack and bedroll, his straggly beard,
sometimes his supermarket cart, he scuttles off
when I show up; more a shadow than a man.

January 20

scouring pans …
snow disappearing
from the yard

January 21

day dreaming …
streaks of rain
on the window

January 22

breathing …
waiting for my
tea to cool down

January 23

doorbell rings!
oh … just the
cable guy

January 24

mask workshop
with Jungian therapist
same old stuff

January 25

important meetings
to discuss the
meaning of things
not for me

January 26

writing a poem
I am quintessentially
alone

January 27

I look up
from writing
to sunlight

January 28

letting
the cat out
the moon in

January 29

gray day ...
hair in the
shower drain
the colour
of winter rain

January 30

recent photos
of myself ...
some I keep
some I throw away

January 31

Mid-day snowfall ... I stand
for a while on the front porch,
looking, breathing ice wine,
alive in the northern air.

Mid-day sunshine ... I stand
for a while on the patio out back,
marveling at the powder blue
and pink clouds, the slice of light
glowing like ripe canteloupe
low in the sky.

I walk around the old neighbor-
hood where everything is new
for an hour or two.

February 1

When I am old, I will be
rather like one of Aunt Clara's
kitchen chairs, I suspect.
Fine wood faded; still
quite sturdy, supporting
family at the table.

I could also be like the old leather
chair in the living room, slumped
and warm and solid, facing the
window, looking south, rocking
in the sun.

February 2

My sister's cat died
but she left the little step
by the cat door in place ...
just because.

February 3

I can't remember what happened
yesterday. Or the day before.
To be honest, it will take me
a while to remember what happened
today, in any detail. But like one of those
rare and vivid dreams we never forget,
I remember 1958. If, fifty years from now
I could look back to today, I wonder
what the dream would be?

February 4

Again, no e-mail
from the editor.
Hard not to imagine
rejection.

February 5

Signing papers at the bank, "there
and there, and there." Virtual money
shuffling around; all some kind of
illusion. Nothing changes outwardly,
except maybe the marker on the security
scale moves from six point five to seven,
temporarily.

Another illusion. There is no security.
And no money. Just numbers on a
computer screen. We continue to
live our lives exactly the way we
would have lived them anyway.

February 6

All poets know that life
is sweeter when death
is close at hand. Part
of the poet's job is to
impart this awareness
to everyone else,
so that everyone else
will know it too.
Trouble is, no one
reads poetry anymore.

February 7

the last leaf
on the oak tree
falls right beside
my rake

February 8

camelias, daffodils,
tulips … don't be
so eager to rush
into bloom

February 9

back stairs
hot sun
cold wind
I understand
baked Alaska

February 10

stooping
I pick up
a tiny white feather
and release it into
the wind ...
it drifts away
south by southwest

February 11

I remember my son
learning to walk.
Today he carries
my groceries
up the stairs.

February 12

Spring flowers
from the market ...
couldn't wait
for Valentine's.

February 13

There are at least a thousand
oak trees in the grove on the hill
near my house. At this point
in the cycle of the seasons,
they are completely and finally
stripped of their leaves, exposed
to the naked eye like contorted
dancers frozen in place, hard,
dense, rigid, incredibly heavy.
At the same time, they are elegant,
delicate, graceful, sinuous, fluid
and light, constantly in motion,
even when the wind is still.

I stand at the summit and imagine
the moving forest of Macbeth,
druids round the fire, hooded
acolytes in single file gliding
through the night.
I have seen folk dancers up there,
and students of the martial arts,
posturing, much like the trees

themselves, and once a Sunday samurai
with a silver sword doing his best
Toshiro Mifune impersonation
for an audience of one.

February 14

My friend is too
busy being a big
business typhoon
to go for a walk.

February 15

Irritable day.
I am preoccupied
with blaming others.
Too bad; the moon
is full tonight.

February 16

Good news and bad.
The magazine editor
still loves me but
the prissy little clerk
at the car insurance
office does not.
Guess which one
I am still thinking about.

February 17

Rummaging through
souvenirs of past glories …
all my blue ribbons
faded to gray.

February 18

My father's paintings
become more beautiful
with each passing year.

February 19

Buried in the drawer
a favourite card
from my daughter.
"The nice thing about
being mean and ugly,"
it says, "is nobody
will notice the change
as you get older."
Happy Birthday!

February 20

Trash day.
I run outside
in my slippers
carrying two bags.
Too late.

February 21

The mail man
brings more bills
and fresh mud
for the porch.

February 22

Impatient driver
honks at me
from behind.
We give each other
the finger.

February 23

Hard to imagine 1915,
the year my mother
was born. Before
the war to end all wars
was over; before the
execution of the Czar,
a quarter century before
I was born. Today,
my mother's ninety-
second birthday, I drive
her downtown and wait
while she gets her hair
done. Afterwards,
we are irritable with
each other, but as always,
it passes. Same old,
same really old.

February 24

mild day ...
driving with the car
window wide open
first time this year.

February 25

soccer players
on the dry field ...
but I have
the wet one
to myself.

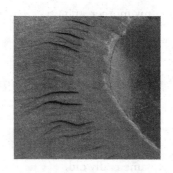

February 26

The last little sheet
of ice screams as I
sweep it away.
The frozen toenails
of winter have been
clipped, and spring
stands poised to dance
over the cold blue hills
sometime soon.

February 27

On the sidewalk someone
calls my name. I turn and stare;
I don't recognize her. But then I do.
An old friend I haven't seen for years.
Her hair is shorter and has turned to gray;
she has lost a lot of weight.
"Dorothy!" I exclaim in surprise.
"You look like yourself!"

February 28

Thursday … a day without …
what? Character? Charisma?
Not quite the beginning and
not quite the end. Probably
the most pallid day of the week.

Thursday is the space between
the notes in a sleepy symphony,
the space between rocks and
shrubs in an old Japanese garden.

I know the spaces are as important
as the things they separate.
It's just that today, Thursday,
I want things, and not spaces.
Do you mind?

February 29

Flowers and freezing
overnight. New life
and the icy pinch of death.
How can this be?
Of course ... last day
of February.

March 1

The first day of
the bitchiest month
of the year. Eliot said
April is the cruelest month
and I know what he means;
every spring, I expect April
to come along and save me
from myself. But I don't expect
any such thing from March.

March 2

"Welcome to Lost Wages!"
rasps the Latino customs officer
with the black moustache.
As a middle-aged Caucasian
Canadian with an English name,
I guess I don't look like a terrorist.
But my shoes must be x-rayed
all the same.

March 3

High-end brand name designer
shops along the psuedo-Graeco-
Roman mall, gleaming aquariums
of glass and platinum with turquoise
and magenta indirect lighting,

two anorexic models posing as
salesgirls, one slim young manager
in an Italian suit and twelve items
for sale displayed like sculpture
in an exclusive gallery.

That hand-bag alone from Milan,
which I know my wife would like,
costs four times as much as the entire
trip so far, including air fare.
Don't you just love that word:
"exclusive." It shuts almost
everybody out, including me.

March 4

If only her ex hadn't shown up drunk
on that rainy night, taken a wild swing
at me and fallen blubbering in the mud.
If only she hadn't dumped me while I was
travelling in Spain. If only she hadn't got
pregnant and told her parents all about it.
If only she hadn't followed me up north,
and got a job in the same small town.
If only she hadn't slept with the lead singer
and run off to Australia. If only she hadn't
terrified me with stories about her father
driving around the city in his black Cadillac
with a gun, looking for us.
If only she hadn't ...

March 5

Buying wine
why do I dither?
I know what I want.
But there's something
about all those beautiful
bottles: blue sky fantasies
of food and golden
vineyards in the sun.
Italy; South Africa;
New Zealand; Argentina.
"Can I help you, sir?"
the sales clerk calls.
Startled, I make my
choices and bumble off
into the dishwater afternoon.

March 6

New local tourism slogan:
"Your search for the perfect
orgasm is over."
All I wanted
was a crumpet
and a cup of tea.

March 7

I don't like the way
I look in this clothing
store mirror.
I wonder if they
have another one?

March 8

shaving in the shower …
three drops of blood
swirl down the drain …
cut myself again.

March 9

red spot on my shoulder
may be cancer says my doctor.
waiting for the biopsy
imagination runs amuck.
but I'm in luck ...
it's just a mole.

March 10

Lunch at my friend's house ...
intimate details about
our private lives exchanged
over curried chicken and rice
go in one ear and out the other.

March 11

My friend lends me
a book on the zen
of creativity.
Let's see ...
page one:
"We don't know
that we are already
what we are trying
to be."

Oh dear. Off to a
slow start.

March 12

Page 242 ... Master Hakuin says,
"If you listen to my teachings
and think you understand zen
then I have failed. If everything
goes well, you will never
understand it."

Oh ... now I get it.

March 13

Closing my eyes, I choose a page
at random in my book of Japanese
death poems, written by zen monks
and haiku poets on the verge of
reincarnation. And here it is ...
page two hundred and thirty-nine,
written by Mabutsu, who died
at seventy-nine on the fifteenth
day of the ninth month, 1874,
the day of the full autumn moon.

Moon in a barrel:
You never know just when
the bottom will fall out.

Those old Japanese poets
will find any excuse
to write about the moon.

March 14

The butt-end of winter
weighs on me like a wool
sweater soaked in a heavy rain.
Where is my sense of humour?
Hanging in the basement
on the drying rack.

March 15

My hands on her warm back
with its spray of tiny freckles.
My fingers on her spine,
kundalini link between
her backside and her brain.
My thumbs in the red zone
between her shoulder blades,
my palms across the Lumbar Plain.
We end up in Thorassic Park,
where ancient aches and pains
lie deep beneath the skin.

March 16

another block ...
now at last the wind
has blown the clouds
apart ... a glimpse
of the stars and the
first quarter moon.

March 17
(3 computer haiku)

I have established
a fragile toehold
on the dark continent
of my computer.

March 18

Autistic machine!
with an impenetrable
mind of its own.

March 19

Wrong key.
What was is no more
and cannot be recovered.

March 20

Fortune cookies …
I don't read them
anymore. Every day
now I bake my own.

March 21

My daughter passes by
on her way to a memorial
for her friend's stillborn baby.
The girls of not so long ago
from the age of innocence
come together to share
the grief and see to it
once more that the circle,
though stretched very wide,
will not be broken. For them,
as for us all, the tears will fall
as we think about what might
have been, what is, and what
is yet to come.

March 22

Talking about the meaning
of life with my friend
on this bright green day,
we fail to notice that
it is snowing outside.

March 23

Such dreams
I've been having!
But I'm not sharing them.
People would laugh and say,
"You made that up!"

March 24

Of the four of us gathered
for lunch, three of us dream
of the reaper on the golf course
right next door. We've heard him
out there in the dead of night,
putting in the gloom.

March 25

"Well, what is it today?"
my Chinese physiotherapist

asks. "Lower back again,"
I say, "right down here."
"Hmmm," she says,
poking and prodding.
"Here's another stretch
for you to do."
She demonstrates;
one foot on the chair,
the other on the floor.
"In China," she says,
"this is called *The idiot
ties his shoe.* Perfect
for you."

March 26

These are the days of death.
Family and friends falling away,
just like in the great stories.
It's partly because this is
the time of our lives, when
we actually have those
dreadful conversations
about our (shooting) pains
and (crippling) aches.

But there's something else
going on, something more
than the normal rate of attrition.
Something dark and sinister
is unfolding, rolling across
the city like a London fog.

March 27

early spring rain
pretty girl
yawning
in the coffee shop

March 28

a wan smile
on the half moon
waning

March 29

streams of pink
confetti in the wind ...
cherry blossoms

March 30

My relationship
with my father
has improved
dramatically
since he died.

March 31

Another gray day
she sighed, looking off
into the middle distance,
seeing only the clouds
and a solitary seagull
falling from the sky
like a stricken kite.

April 1

It took him a minute to understand
where he was ... he first became
aware of the fire ... and the light
seeping through the window ...
then the geometry of the house
revealed itself to him. He saw
her through the half-open door
to the bedroom ... she was bending
smoothing the sheets or some such
humble domestic chore and he was
struck by a soft lightning bolt of
desire sharp and sweet.

He closed the door
he closed his eyes
he fell asleep ...

he had a dream ...
or was it a dream?
looking back now
he couldn't be sure.

April 2

I'm all on edge
waiting for you.
I think I see you
everywhere ...
across the street
over there
standing talking to
a pair of strangers
walking with that slut
all dressed in black.

Please hurry back ...
I'm freezing on this
godforsaken corner.

April 3

Rain drops
on the watering can ...
irritating noise.

April 4

She goes away
for a couple of days ...
camelia blossoms
on the ground.

April 5

A mysterious shift
in the visual plane ...
suddenly sunshine.

April 6

I am wrestling gingerly
with the gargoyle of pain
who has taken up residence
in my lower right back.
I have to engage him gently,
lovingly, even, before he will
release me from the rack.
It's been a long time now,
and he doesn't seem ready
to move on. I am defeated,
on the edge of surrender.
Maybe this will help.

April 7

New moon poised
like a golden blade
above the horizon.
New season pouring
cold and sharp
like ice wine.

After enlightenment
the moon is just
the moon, and spring
is spring again.

April 8

I went for a walk
around the neighborhood
looking for a poem.

I paid attention
to what was
going on.

To the pain
in my back,
beginning to ease
(oh please, God!).

To the sound
of my own slow

steps rising from
the sodden ground.

To the flocks
of ecstatic birds
dashing from
tree to tree.

To the fathers
calling children.

To the joyous hymn
rising from within
the corner church.

A good neighborhood,
no doubt. But a slow
day for poems.

April 9

I know something about you.
And I'll tell you what it is
in just a moment.
It's something very important.
Very big. Very deep. Very private.
It's based on my complete faith
in my intuition, which never fails me
in these matters. You will be tempted
to brush aside this observation of mine,
this truth about you. Don't just dismiss

it as shallow sentimental nonsense;
take a moment and look below the
surface; go for the story beneath
the story; stay open; put your inner
critic on hold.

Are you ready? Okay … here it is.
The truth is, you're amazing!
No, I mean truly! Trust me on this.
Don't move away; come back here.
I'm speaking from the heart.
I'm saying this because it's long
overdue, and I need to say it.
Look me right in the eye, if you can.

You're magical! You're so much fun
to be with! I've seen you at your best,
absolutely dazzling. You know this
about yourself, don't you. Yes, you do.
In your secret heart, you know how
great it is to be you, to be with you;
what fabulous company you are.
You've got so much love in you;
you're smart, you're funny, you're
sensitive, generous and kind.
You're a warm and passionate lover.

But you've denied it for so long
you've almost lost it. And you want
somebody to see this in you,
really see this. And I have.
Just a glimpse was all I needed.

April 10

Intimations of innocence
come, when they come at all,
in sudden tremors of recognition,
shivers of ecstatic energy from
somewhere south of the heart.
They are so elusive they slip
through your consciousness
like light on the lip of a waterfall.
And you can't just conjure them
up again once they're gone.
You have to wait for another
spontaneous opening of the
crown chakra, when memories
and feelings will pour through you
like a skein of tiny falling stars.

April 11

Watching Audrey Hepburn
and William Holden cavorting
in Paris, I am briefly transported
to a dream time, when fountains
and fireworks splashed and exploded
in glittering silver cascades, love was
in the air, violins played, and everywhere
champagne laughter rose over the
happy mob in the crowded square.

I am a child of the time
when such dreams were made,

and a child I have remained,
smiling like a simpleton
in front of the tube
while the band plays on.

April 12

sunny day ...
full circle
another spring
swings by
she is tentative
at first, then
bold and bright
a gangly young
goddess with
spiky hair
pale skin
and long legs
wearing yellow
and pink and green.
I am father to this
dazzling daughter
of the earth.

April 13

Today, out of the basement
and into the sun came the little
ceramic tai-chi man, the concrete
garden gargoyle, the fabric wind fish
and the bamboo wind chimes.
Each is returned to its place:
tai-chi master beside the pond;
wind fish hanging from the cherry tree;
gargoyle crouching in the daffodils;
wind chimes dangling from the oak.
Humble possessions, childlike pleasures.
Sometimes it's enough.

April 14

"Well, now that I've got you
both together, I can tell you,"
my daughter says to my wife
and me. Brief pause.
The afternoon light streams
through the window;
the refrigerator hums.
I become aware that
I have stopped breathing.
"I'm pregnant," she says,
smiling, leaning expectantly
on the counter. Hugs all around
and eyes shiny with tears.
Then I am heading down

the hall to the den to be alone
for a moment. I just need
to be alone for a moment
and say some kind of prayer.

Three poems after Tachibana Akami
(1812-68)
"Poems of Solitary Delights"

April 15

What a delight it is
when facing a blank
page to take my pen
and find the words
still waiting for me.

April 16

What a delight it is
in the morning garden
to find a flower in full
bloom that was not there
yesterday.

April 17

What a delight it is
when writing a new story
to find I have created
a character who is
not at all like me.

April 18

With the west wind
a gentle goddess came.
She soaked the wood,
she soaked the sundial
she soaked the raccoons
hiding under the bamboo.
Secretly, she soaked
the cathedral in the heart
of town; she soaked
the harbour, the theatre,
the cricket pitch in the
park beside the sea.
With the west wind
the gentle goddess
blew away … after
a day or two of rain.

April 19

Out of sorts
I return from town.
Then, in the garden,
the cherry tree.

April 20

Dejected and tired
I come in from the wind.
Then, in the living room,
the music.

April 21

Irritated ... I wait.
My friend is late
for lunch. Then,
in the restaurant,
the hot tea.

April 22

This wild weather and my friend's
continuing self-absorption, put me
in mind of hexagram number four
from the I Ching, "Youthful Folly,"
which speaks of spring gushing
from the earth, running everywhere,
not having chosen a path, but alive
and flowing on, naïve energy
in full early bloom.

The oracle comments:
"Seek sound advice
and set limitations.

The excesses of immaturity
are wearisome and exhaust
the good will of friends."

April 23

Dark feelings from the past
flow through me again,
like an old addiction
that started off brilliant
and dreamlike, only to end
in heartache and despair
in the so-called light of day.
Maybe projection is the way
to go after all, in the Jungian
sense, I mean.

April 24

I sit and struggle
to describe the
indescribable.
The tao that can
be described is
not the tao
and all that.

But I did it once
last week - described
the tao, I mean.

But no matter how
hard I try right now
I can't seem to do it again.

April 25

It was a time when
we lived in a small town
in a big valley, sheltered
from the outside world by
dense forests, high mountains,
bad roads, lack of money,
clunky cars. We were rubes
in the rough, home boys happy
on the dusty baseball diamond
behind the old high school.

Just a few years, a precious
few years, childhood. Long enough
to build the foundation and frame
of a dream. A time when mountains
were just mountains, to be climbed,
not contemplated.

April 26

Drive to the paint store
and buy the wrong paint.
Drive back in heavy traffic
and buy the right stuff.

April 27

She calls from work.
Drive there and back
in heavy traffic.
Forgot her keys
and glasses.

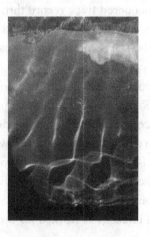

April 28

Drive to the restaurant
to buy a gift certificate.
Eleven o'clock; not open
yet. Drive home in heavy
traffic and throw in the towel.
The feng shui of this week
is way out of alignment.

April 29

My friend's son graduated
at the top of his class
the other day, up at the university,
standing head and shoulders
above most of his classmates,
literally and metaphorically.
Of course, he's a little older,
having racked up an impressively
chequered track record through
his twenties with crappy old cars,
false starts and abandoned careers,
busted in California, coming home
broke, with big debts and no prospects,
too much dope and bad company.
I congratulated him on becoming
an adult, because I know how hard
it is, and I told him not to worry
because he could still act wild
sometimes and make an ass
of himself. It worked for me.

April 30

I'm not the sort of person who
goes to cemeteries. Except for
the one on Josephine Street,
up near the old Gill School.
It's just a field, really, surrounded
by trees, with long grass turning
yellow here and there amongst
the faded gray headstones.
I walk down the path that leads to
my aunt's grave, a simple plaque,
set in the ground, polished marble,
brown and white. I brush away
the grass and weeds and clean the
little space with her names, which
reverberate through my heart and
memory on this last day of
the sweetest month of spring.

Her names are my names,
the foundation stones of my
invisible self, one thing that never
changes in my life. Next, beside
the grave I place some wild flowers
I have picked over by the fence, yellow,
blue and red, and stand breathing deeply,
head spinning in the afternoon sun.
I step into the shade beneath the tree,
close my eyes, and return along the
timeline to the big house on River Road.
The cooling breeze carries me down
the way to 1952, to the lilac bush by

the back stair, the porch, the kitchen
itself, the living room, the green wooden
swing in the garden out by the maple tree.
The people are all in their places,
eating and laughing, playing cards
on the long winter nights, growing
old together, dying and moving on.
Intimate details about folks dead
over fifty years are so clear it could
have been just the other day: smells,
coughs, shoes, cigarette-stained fingers,
sheet music on the grand piano,
fresh-cut firewood, quirks and foibles,
earrings and Christmas tree decorations.
I remember it all, in a kind of fluid rush,
my internal camera gliding from room
to room, across the big yard and garden,
out into the orchard and the fields of
potatoes, cabbage and corn.

I know I'm finished when I open
my eyes and start to move away.
I am tired and full, having drunk
deeply from the well of reincarnation.
At the same time, I am empty.
I walk back along the path to my car,
listening only to the birds and the wind.

Time for me to go. Reluctantly,
I drive away. "See you all of a sudden!"
my aunt calls, and in my imagination
waves to me, just the way she used to.

May 1

I am stalling, procrastinating,
dithering, waiting for just
the right moment, the tipping
point, the peak of the apex,
as my father used to say,
when the critical mass of
the see-saw tilts my way
and I can return to solid ground,
stand up and walk on, a little
shaky perhaps, but moving
beyond jumping up and down
on the spot, toward the next
set of probabilities. Today,
out of the gray doldrums
of indecision, a poem arises.
I embrace it gratefully.

May 2

My how time flies when you're writing poems.
And if you're going to write a poem a day
for a year, you have to spend a lot of time
in "the moment," the holy grail of the eastern
schools of meditation, the absolute essence
of being right here, right now, not thinking
about not thinking, and not thinking about
anything in particular. Except a poem,
perhaps, if you're writing poetry every day.
Because poems are lurking in the moment,

and like an angler heading for the fishing hole,
I return to the moment, carrying my fishing rod,
at least once a day. If you love fishing
or writing poems, you will know how time
flies if you do it every day for a year,
and you will know that a year goes by
in a moment ... just like that!

Photo by Daniel Sikorskyi

Ellery Littleton lives in Victoria, BC.
His previous books include *Old Rocks,
New Streams — 64 Poems from the I Ching —*
and *Time Crimes*, a novel.

Both are available from Trafford
Publishing: www.trafford.com